Seeing the Good in Students

A Guide to Classroom Discipline in Middle School

From **Responsive Classroom**®

with Rashid Abdus-Salaam ■ Andy Moral ■ Kathleen Wylie

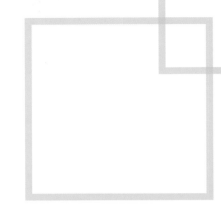

All net proceeds from the sale of this book support the work of Center for Responsive Schools, Inc., a not-for-profit educational organization and the developer of the *Responsive Classroom*® approach to teaching.

Many of the stories in this book are based on real events. To respect students' privacy, names and identifying characteristics of the students and situations have been changed.

ISBN: 978-1-892989-93-2
Library of Congress Control Number: 2018963547

Classroom photographs by Jeff Woodward

Center for Responsive Schools, Inc.
85 Avenue A, P.O. Box 718
Turners Falls, MA 01376-0718

800-360-6332
www.responsiveclassroom.org

Third printing 2021

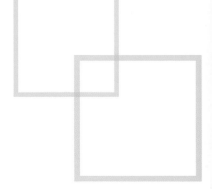

Contents

Overview of the *Responsive Classroom®* Approach to Discipline

Imagine a bustling seventh grade science classroom in the midst of small group experiments. As students collaborate, the room is filled with the sounds of learning. The teacher, Mrs. Smith, sees Marcus and Robin fooling around with some of the equipment. She walks over and asks them, "How should you be using the beakers?" Marcus and Robin set the beakers down carefully and get back to work. Meanwhile, across the room, Derek and Janelle are disagreeing about how best to document their experiment. Feeling himself get frustrated, Derek walks to the window and takes a moment to cool down by doing some deep breathing exercises. As Mrs. Smith continues circulating and observing the groups, she sees Anya, Jaylen, and Cameron hard at work. "I notice you're about halfway through your experiment. What have you discovered so far?" she asks them, and listens with enthusiasm to their response. In short, this is a well-managed classroom in which students can work together and learning can thrive.

This vision of harmonious, productive classroom life is within reach when students learn self-control and the other social-emotional skills they need to successfully collaborate and learn. The *Responsive Classroom* approach to discipline is designed to teach students these skills and to instill the desire to choose responsible behavior because students see the value in doing so rather than being motivated by external factors. Instead of giving out prizes for good behavior, handing down harsh punishments for misbehavior, or offering vague directives such as "Stop it" or "That's enough," teachers using this approach set clear expectations and help students build the understanding and the skills they need to meet those expectations.

Just as the word "discipline" is derived from the Latin word for learning, this approach is grounded in the beliefs that students can learn to be self-regulating, cooperative, caring, and responsible; that we teach discipline just as we teach any content area; and that students learn best when they're actively engaged and invested in constructing their own understanding. Much as we might teach a student to play the flute or graph variables, we must teach students expectations for behavior and give them opportunities to practice in order to find success.

This is not a new style of discipline. Since 1981, thousands of teachers have used it as part of the *Responsive Classroom* approach to teaching. The primary goals of this type of discipline are to:

1 Be kind yet firm so that students feel respected and encouraged

2 Build and maintain feelings of belonging and significance

3 Be effective in the long term at helping students control their behavior

4 Teach social and emotional skills

5 Help students use their personal power in positive ways

Teachers who use this approach take time to get to know students and their social and academic goals. These teachers also spend time discussing how the classroom or school rules can help everyone meet their goals. Although there will always be times when students don't enjoy following the rules or choose not to do so, this approach can help students see the rules in a positive way overall.

In order to achieve the goals listed above, the techniques and practices described in this book meet three criteria:

■ **They are clear and respectful.** The practices teachers use under the *Responsive Classroom* approach come from a place of high expectations and the belief that students can meet those expectations. We set clear guidelines to help students understand what to do, and when we implement discipline practices, we do so calmly, professionally, and with empathy for students.

■ **They help students feel a sense of belonging and significance.** To be fully engaged in classroom life, students need to have a sense of connection with others and also to feel that they are known and appreciated as individuals. Even when a student chooses not to follow the rules, they should be treated as a member of the classroom community who simply needs additional support.

■ **They teach skills to build social-emotional competencies.** Often, students may not follow the rules because they don't yet have the skills to do so. Teaching social-emotional skills, whether through an explicit lesson or by embedding them into academic content, is an important way to help students learn how to meet expectations and behave in a way that supports their success.

Common Styles of Teacher Leadership

Think back on how you experienced discipline when you were a young adolescent. Whether we embrace or reject the approach to discipline we experienced, that approach often influences our own style. We may also be influenced by our background as an educator, our school's approach to discipline, and factors such as constraints on time and the resources at our disposal. No matter what our approach to discipline looks like, it likely fits into one of the following teacher leadership styles.

An Autocratic Style: "Just do what I say."

Often characterized by rules that are stated in the negative ("Don't talk without raising your hand") and presented without discussion, the implicit belief of this style is that students are naturally unruly and impulsive. The rules, therefore, are aimed at keeping them quiet and obedient. This is the teaching style many of us experienced as students, so it can feel intuitive to use this style ourselves. We may believe that if we don't strictly enforce the rules, students will run wild in class, jumping out of their seats, yelling to friends across the room, and throwing materials around.

A drawback of the autocratic leadership style is that rather than assessing whether students understand the rules, it is primarily concerned with whether or not students follow them. Students are compelled to follow the rules mainly out of fear of what will happen if they don't. For many students, this means following the rules only when the teacher and the possibility of punishment are present, and disregarding the rules when the teacher is not there to enforce them. An autocratic style can cause some students to become defiant or resistant to rules whose purposes have not been clearly explained, while other students cling so completely to the rules that, without an adult to guide their behavior, they are unable to make decisions.

This style can create an orderly classroom, but at a cost. Enforcing compliance rather than teaching self-control can result in students feeling anxious, resentful, or angry. Punitive teaching strategies can also lead to students blaming external factors for their behavior rather than taking responsibility for themselves. So, while an autocratic style may produce a calm classroom—at least in the teacher's presence—it does so at the expense of students' dignity and social-emotional development.

A Permissive Style: "Could you please follow the rules?"

The opposite extreme is a leadership style that sets no clear limits for students' behavior. In classrooms where this style is used, expectations are not consistently enforced. Even if the rules are clearly stated and prominently posted in the classroom, students know those rules are negotiable.

Teachers using a permissive style may have experienced an autocratic teaching style when they were students and don't want to put their own students through a similar experience. Teachers using this style also may place a lot of importance on students liking them and might be concerned that being too hard on students will alienate them. As a result, they may hesitate to respond firmly and clearly to misbehavior. Or they may believe that the best way to influence students' behavior is to reinforce good behavior with liberal praise or bribe students to behave with external rewards, all the while ignoring undesirable behavior in the hopes that if it's ignored, the behavior will simply stop.

Regardless of intention, a permissive style can be detrimental to learning for a number of reasons. Left unchecked, small problems balloon into larger disturbances, unresolved conflicts undermine the learning community, and unaddressed teasing and taunting cause students to feel physically and psychologically unsafe. Students who do follow the rules often do so not out of an intrinsic desire to do what's right but to win the approval of their teacher.

The effect of this lack of structure and clear boundaries can resemble the results of an autocratic teaching style—students who are fearful, tense, and dependent. As counterintuitive as it may seem, having too much freedom can cause students a great deal of anxiety as they attempt to determine exactly what is expected of them and where the limits are.

Teachers, too, can feel exhausted by this approach, holding so little authority that they often resort to pleading and bribing to convince students to cooperate. Consistently relying on external rewards can lessen students' intrinsic motivation to follow the rules, which creates a negative cycle in which student motivation decreases as the teacher's pleas and bribery increase. Teachers using this style may grow so discouraged that they end up experiencing burnout.

A Flip-Flop Style: "Stop it. Okay, you have one more chance. All right, that's enough!"

A third leadership style bounces back and forth between autocratic and permissive extremes, often without warning. This may be the most difficult approach for teachers and students alike: teachers swing wildly between punishment and begging or bribery, and students don't know which to expect. A teacher employing this style might ignore students using their phones during one class period, hoping that students will correct the behavior on their own, then berate students the next day for the same behavior. This lack of predictability and consistency leads students to feel confused, frustrated, and anxious.

A lack of experience or administrative support often contributes to this style. A new teacher's best intentions can be undermined by inexperience once they're in front of a class full of students with different needs and varying levels of social-emotional skills. Even if a teacher has learned about classroom management while earning their degree, the reality of overseeing dozens of students, some of whom they only see for one period a day, can challenge the sincerest of intentions. This challenge is compounded when the school's administration lacks the staff or resources to offer support or if similar behavior expectations are not being reinforced throughout the school. However, even experienced and well-supported teachers can find themselves using this style as they work to maintain control of their classroom if they are unaware of a different way.

IN THE CLASSROOM

Throughout this book, you'll get real-world advice and points of view from teachers experienced in using the *Responsive Classroom* approach. See page 11 to meet them!

Mrs. Wylie

Mrs. Wylie has found a noticeable decrease in discipline issues since she started using the *Responsive Classroom* approach. In her estimation, ninety percent of the behavior issues in her classroom are handled proactively through making community expectations clear and creating a predictable and safe environment. Students with an unpredictable life outside of school respond especially well to a classroom where they know what to expect each day and what is expected of them.

The *Responsive Classroom* Style of Teacher Leadership

The *Responsive Classroom* teacher leadership style laid out in this book offers a productive alternative. This style is neither autocratic nor permissive, but authoritative. It comes from a place of empathy and a belief in students' desire to do what's right. Instead of relying on punishment or rewards to influence students' behavior, the authoritative approach helps students build and practice self-control, understand what socially responsible behavior is, and see the ways such behavior benefits both themselves and others.

In an authoritative leadership style, teachers strive to be firm, kind, and consistent. The goal is to develop a calm, safe, and orderly classroom where students can do their best learning. We do this by helping students become aware of how their actions have consequences—both positive and negative—for themselves and those around them. When a student misbehaves, a respectful but firm response that preserves the dignity of the student can help stop the misbehavior as quickly as possible so that an atmosphere of learning can be restored.

An authoritative leadership style considers the needs of both the group and the individual. It balances the requirement for order with students' need for interactive and social learning, as well as balancing the need for teachers to be in control

◼ IN THE CLASSROOM

Mr. Moral

Before learning the *Responsive Classroom* approach, Mr. Moral used an autocratic teaching style that resembled what he experienced as a young adolescent. Fear of punishment compelled him to follow the rules, so he in turn used punishment to motivate students. These punishments, such as excluding students from recess, class parties, or other fun events, were often unrelated to the actual misbehavior. He would also try to coerce students into following the rules by responding to misbehavior with a harsh tone of voice and language. While this caused most students to comply, more and more behavior issues arose as the year went on. Because students weren't learning how to monitor and control their own behavior, Mr. Moral observed frequent negative interactions among peers and between students and teachers.

After his first year of teaching, Mr. Moral was introduced to the *Responsive Classroom* approach and started using a teaching style focused on proactive discipline. Over the years, this shift has resulted in of the classroom with the need for students to control their own learning. For this balancing act to work, teachers must get to know their students individually, culturally, and developmentally and take the time to teach students the skills they need to be contributing members of a productive and inclusive learning community.

All too often, students are expected to enter middle school having already mastered the social skills necessary for success. But just as we don't expect students to come to school already understanding basic algebra or how to write a persuasive essay, teachers using an authoritative approach understand that students need to practice social-emotional skills in order to become more adept. Some students will arrive with more highly developed social skills on the first day of school, while others will need extra support to develop those skills. Teachers using an authoritative approach understand that as students develop, they will all need to continuously develop and refine those skills through practice.

School provides abundant opportunities for students to practice the social and behavioral skills they need to be successful as they enter adolescence and their adult personalities begin to take shape. Whether they are learning to collaborate on a project with a partner, welcome a new student into the class, or respectfully disagree with a classmate during a debate, school is an ideal setting for students to learn to think and act in socially responsible ways.

more positive interactions and relationships with students—and parents*—and in students' developing the ability to self-regulate their behavior and emotions on a consistent basis.

Since adopting an authoritative approach to teaching discipline, Mr. Moral takes plenty of time early in the year to teach and model academic routines and behaviors as well as social behaviors. The time and energy he spends preparing students for appropriate behavior means less time and energy spent on responding to misbehavior later on.

*About the Term "Parent"

Many students are being raised by grandparents, siblings, aunts and uncles, foster families, and other caregivers. All of these individuals are to be honored for devoting their time, attention, and love to raising children. In this book, for ease of reading, the term "parent" is used to represent all the caregivers involved in a student's life.

The *Responsive Classroom* Discipline Framework

In the chapters that follow, you will learn proactive strategies for establishing clear behavior expectations and teaching students how to meet those expectations. You will also learn strategies for responding to misbehavior in ways that preserve the dignity of the student and allow for learning to continue with as few interruptions as possible.

Students' ability to control their behavior relies on their social and emotional skills, which are still developing. Center for Responsive Schools, the developer of the *Responsive Classroom* approach, bases all of its programs on the belief that in order for students to achieve success both in and out of school, they need to

Social-Emotional Competencies

Center for Responsive Schools
Cooperation—Students' ability to establish new relationships, maintain positive relationships and friendships, avoid social isolation, resolve conflicts, accept differences, be a contributing member of the classroom and school community, and work productively and collaboratively with others.
Assertiveness—Students' ability to take initiative, stand up for their ideas without hurting or negating others, seek help, succeed at a challenging task, and recognize their individual self as separate from the circumstances or conditions they're in.
Responsibility—Students' ability to motivate themselves to take action and follow through on expectations; to define a problem, consider the consequences, and choose a positive solution.
Empathy—Students' ability to "see into" (recognize, understand) another's state of mind and emotions and be receptive to new ideas and perspectives; to appreciate and value differences and diversity in others; to have concern for others' welfare, even when it doesn't benefit or may come at a cost to one's self.
Self-Control—Students' ability to recognize and regulate their thoughts, emotions, and behaviors in order to be successful in the moment and remain on a successful trajectory.

learn five specific social and emotional competencies. These align with the five core social-emotional competencies outlined by the Collaborative for Academic, Social, and Emotional Learning (CASEL) as a means of promoting intrapersonal, interpersonal, and cognitive competence (n.d.).

As teachers, it is important for us to both help students strengthen these competencies directly and to model them ourselves. Seeing how adults demonstrate these competencies sends a powerful message to young adolescents and helps them envision how they can practice healthy behaviors now and as they develop. That's especially important during early adolescence, when students are beginning to form their adult identities and need strong role models.

The *Responsive Classroom* discipline framework (see the following page) is based upon the goal of helping students develop these competencies. This framework includes five key components, each with a set of goals for teachers.

CASEL

Relationship Skills—The ability to establish and maintain healthy and rewarding relationships with diverse individuals and groups. The ability to communicate clearly, listen well, cooperate with others, resist inappropriate social pressure, negotiate conflict constructively, and seek and offer help when needed.

Self-Awareness—The ability to accurately recognize one's own emotions, thoughts, and values and how they influence behavior. The ability to accurately assess one's strengths and limitations, with a well-grounded sense of confidence, optimism, and a growth mindset.

Responsible Decision-Making—The ability to make constructive choices about personal behavior and social interactions based on ethical standards, safety concerns, and social norms. The realistic evaluation of consequences of various actions, and a consideration of the well-being of oneself and others.

Social Awareness—The ability to take the perspective of and empathize with others, including those from diverse backgrounds and cultures. The ability to understand social and ethical norms for behavior and to recognize family, school, and community resources and supports.

Self-Management—The ability to successfully regulate one's emotions, thoughts, and behaviors in different situations, effectively managing stress, controlling impulses, and motivating oneself. The ability to set and work toward personal and academic goals.

Responsive Classroom Discipline Framework

Component	Goals
Creating a safe and predictable learning environment	To lay the foundation for a safe and positive learning community
Preventing off-task behavior and misbehavior	To establish rules and hold students to those rules in a proactive, firm, fair, and consistent manner
Responding to off-task behavior and misbehavior	To handle off-task behavior and misbehavior respectfully, and to help the student get back on track, repair any damage caused, and develop self-discipline so as to prevent similar problems in the future
Solving chronic behavior problems	To understand the student's particular behavior problem and address it with modified or individualized discipline practices that get the student back on track for developing self-regulation; to help the student learn which strategies for returning to positive behavior work for them
Managing outbursts	To deescalate or interrupt behavioral or emotional outbursts, and to draw upon community support to help a student regain self-control at the point of escalation

This book follows the structure of this discipline framework. The first two chapters focus on how to build a solid foundation for positive behavior by creating a safe learning environment and investing students in the rules. Chapter 3 explains how to help students get back on task when they lose sight of the rules and misbehave, as all students will at some point. The last two chapters address more persistent behavior problems, including those that may be the result of toxic stress.

Through the use of the techniques outlined in this book, you can foster the essential social and emotional competencies students need and create learning environments where they can thrive. The skills students learn now will serve them in their lives both inside and outside the classroom, in the present and for a lifetime.

Voices in This Book

Throughout this book, you'll find examples of the *Responsive Classroom* approach in action in middle school. These examples come from real classrooms where teachers have seen the positive results of this approach, and can help you visualize how you might use the techniques outlined in this book in your own classroom.

Rashid Abdus-Salaam is a consulting teacher for Center for Responsive Schools and an AP geography teacher at Knowledge Academy High School in Nashville, Tennessee. He holds a master's degree in curriculum instruction and a BA in history. Mr. Abdus-Salaam has a great love for the educational theory of cognitive growth through social interactions and a passion for creating opportunities to develop the whole-child learning approach through positive team building.

Andy Moral teaches sixth grade math and science in Bucks County, Pennsylvania, and has also taught sixth grade social studies and language arts. In addition to teaching, Mr. Moral serves as a staff developer in his school district and supports teachers' professional development. He has been practicing and teaching the *Responsive Classroom* approach for over ten years and sees the positive impact the approach has on student learning and school culture.

Kathleen Wylie is passionate about creating authentic, meaningful learning experiences for her diverse student population. Over her 15-year career, she has taught in urban, suburban, and rural settings, and she currently teaches social studies in Schenectady, New York. In 2018, Mrs. Wylie received the Schenectady School District Teacher of the Year award and was a semifinalist for New York State Teacher of the Year. She attributes this success in large part to her work with and commitment to *Responsive Classroom* practices.

Reference

Collaborative for Academic, Social, and Emotional Learning. n.d. "Core SEL Competencies." Accessed July 6, 2018. https://casel.org/core-competencies/.

Building a Foundation for Learning

Building a Foundation for Learning

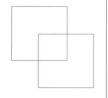

When students walk into a new classroom on the first day of school, all kinds of questions rush through their heads. How hard will this class be? What will the teacher be like? Will any of my friends be in this class? Will I get called on to talk? This uncertainty can be compounded when students change classrooms for each subject, particularly if they are new to middle school and unfamiliar with the process of changing classes.

As social beings, we all crave information about what to expect in unfamiliar situations. Whether starting a new job, joining a new team, or entering a new country, we need to know the customs and codes of conduct in the new environment. Young adolescents, especially, want this kind of information. They are at a natural point in their development to try out different behaviors, make new social connections, and test limits to determine where the boundaries are. Thus, they need clear information about expectations right from the first days of school in order to feel safe and ready to learn.

At the beginning of the year, students are watching us closely as we set the tone for the classroom and the school community. Thus, it's important to emphasize from the start that in this classroom, the expectation is that everyone will behave with respect and kindness. As students test limits, which is to be expected, they need to see you as a calm and steady presence who will hold fast to established expectations and hold everyone accountable in a kind and respectful way. This allows students to feel a sense of comfort and safety, which in turn frees them to participate more actively and engage more fully with learning.

Through the techniques in this chapter, you will learn how to establish this sense of predictability and help students along the path to positive behavior and enthusiastic participation in academics. The ways in which you implement these techniques will vary depending on the subjects you teach, the structure of your teaching team and schedule, and the developmental levels of the students in your classes.

 To learn more about young adolescents' development and how it affects them in the classroom, see *Yardsticks: Child and Adolescent Development Ages 4–14* by Chip Wood (Center for Responsive Schools, 2017).

IN THE CLASSROOM

Mrs. Wylie

When students and their parents come in to meet their teachers before the school year starts, Mrs. Wylie holds a scavenger hunt for them that extends from the classroom throughout the school. This gives students and their parents a chance to get a feel for the classroom and to see where things are located in the school, such as the cafeteria and the bus drop-off.

Mr. Abdus-Salaam

Before the school year starts, Mr. Abdus-Salaam holds a meet-and-greet and ice cream social for students and their parents. He shows a short video from the previous year to introduce his classroom and teacher leadership style and to show what students might expect in the upcoming year. This helps students feel more at ease, and meeting with parents initiates a rapport that Mr. Abdus-Salaam strengthens throughout the year with regular communication and opportunities for them to get involved at school.

Organizing the Classroom for Success

How your classroom is organized and decorated will be one of the first things students notice when they walk in the door. The way furniture and materials are arranged can offer a lot of information about how this class will be and can help create a welcoming atmosphere. Try to picture your classroom through a new student's eyes: When they walk in for the first time, do they see an inviting, well-organized space? Do they see space for them to work, or is the room packed with materials they don't know how to use yet? Are wall displays simple and instructive, or potentially confusing?

From day one, we can send students the message that the classroom is an inclusive and respectful space, that the teacher is in control, and that standards for behavior are high. Areas to display students' work, furniture arranged with adolescent needs in mind, and places for both individual and small group work invite students to engage with the classroom. Here are some tips for creating a classroom that gives students the chance to feel comfortable, understand your expectations for them, and be ready to start learning right from the first day.

■ IN THE CLASSROOM

Mrs. Wylie

The structure of Mrs. Wylie's class underwent a big change when she began exploring a more effective way to arrange desks. Before, she used to switch back and forth between having students sit in rows, facing forward, and having them do partner work. Both had frustrating results: students got restless in rows, and they weren't prepared for the expectations of partner work. But when she tried clusters of four desks, she discovered that having small groups of students facing each other supported collaborative work beautifully. These clusters made it easier for students to see everyone in their group, hear and acknowledge everyone's ideas, and adapt to different collaborative structures, such as table discussions, around-the-circle sharing, and partner chats.

Mr. Moral

Knowing that students this age need a lot of space, Mr. Moral tests out any new seating arrangement prior to assigning seats to ensure that there is enough room between desks for students to sit comfortably, that he can move around the classroom while teaching, and that all students are able to see the board without having to move their chair. He bases seating arrangements on the unit of study. For example, if a unit requires small group interactions, he arranges desks in table groups to facilitate conversation. For a unit that requires more

Furniture

Whether your classroom uses desks, tables, or some combination of the two, certain seating arrangements can maximize learning while minimizing distractions. Having students seated in clusters of three or four can support both partner and small group discussions. Arranging seating so that students can see one another's faces can lead to richer and more involved conversations among peers. In addition, arranging furniture so that partners or groups have a shared surface on which to work helps students work more productively together.

Along with supporting student learning, an effective furniture arrangement can minimize distractions. Arrange

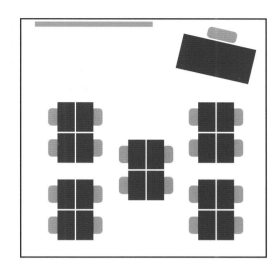

individual work, he arranges desks in rows with enough space between them so that chatting is less of a temptation, but close enough that students can still talk and collaborate when necessary.

Mr. Abdus-Salaam

Mr. Abdus-Salaam arranges his classroom furniture so that students sit in clusters of three to four. Desks are arranged so that no one has their back to the teacher. Aisles created by the clusters are always kept clear and make it easy for students to go get supplies, move to the group meeting area, and enter and leave the classroom.

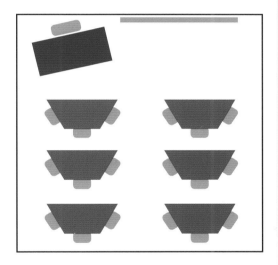

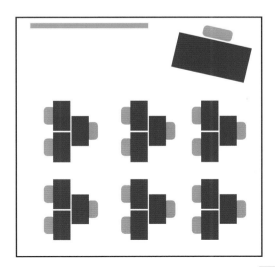

student seating so that there are clear paths between learning clusters, wide enough to accommodate middle school students' growing bodies. Students should be able to enter, exit, and move around the classroom without disrupting their peers' learning.

No matter how you arrange the furniture in your classroom, it may be helpful to assign seats at the beginning of the year. Doing so can help relieve anxiety students may feel about where and with whom to sit. You may also find it useful to have students make name tags or cards as a fun first-day icebreaker and to help everyone learn each other's names. This is a good activity to coordinate with your teaching team. For example, you might decide that all first period classes on the team will take a few minutes at the start of class to create name tags, which all students can then wear for the rest of the day.

Classroom Supplies

Young adolescents crave and benefit from opportunities to practice independence. Although the quantity and type of classroom supplies will vary based on the subject and unit of study, giving students access to frequently used tools and supplies allows them to practice responsibility by independently retrieving items when they're needed, taking proper care of those items, and putting them away when finished using them. Consider labeling the parts of any complex tools or machines

■ IN THE CLASSROOM

Mr. Moral

Mr. Moral's classroom has a designated area for clearly labeled supplies that students may need for activities or projects. When students are seated in table groups, Mr. Moral also places a supply caddy on each table with some commonly needed materials like markers or sticky notes, as well as any special materials required for a particular lesson or unit.

that students might use. This allows students to reinforce their knowledge of relevant tools in an independent and natural way.

Before students start using new supplies or equipment, use Interactive Modeling (see pages 28–32) to teach and model how to properly use, take care of, and put away those supplies. For instance, not only might students need to know how to calibrate a scale, but they also need to understand how to safely carry it from where it is stored to their work area. The same is true of microscopes, chemicals, and other science equipment; instruments and music stands; art supplies; technology and machinery; and physical education equipment. Model how to use a specific item just before using it for the first time in order to set students up for success. As students continue to work with more familiar items, use teacher language (see pages 21–27) to remind students of your expectations.

To facilitate students' independent use of various supplies and materials, be sure to store them neatly and label them clearly. This helps students quickly and easily find what they need, maximizing the time they have to focus on learning. If you have materials that you won't be using until later in the semester or year, consider keeping them in a supply cabinet or otherwise out of sight until you're ready to introduce them. That way, these materials don't become a distraction or clutter the room, and you can ensure that they're used properly. You also might consider showcasing supplies for an upcoming unit by placing them in a special area with a sign that says "Coming attraction!" or something similar. This can help you build excitement while making it clear that these materials are to be used soon—but not yet.

Decor

At the beginning of the year, keep posters and other visual displays to a minimum so that students can see there is room for their contributions. Consider including some empty bulletin boards with titles at the top to help students envision where their work will be displayed later on. A few charts or other visuals may be useful for giving students a glance at the material they'll be learning early in the year or for providing information that they'll need to reference frequently.

■ IN THE CLASSROOM

Mr. Abdus-Salaam

Mr. Abdus-Salaam keeps a table in the back of the room reserved for project displays. Students' completed presentations and models are exhibited there, generally for a couple weeks. These displays enable students to share their work not only with classmates but with students who come to the room for other classes as well, further strengthening the school community.

Mr. Moral

One item Mr. Moral always keeps on display is the chart that shows the goals students are currently working on. This chart is displayed near the list of classroom rules to serve as a reminder of how the rules and goals are linked. He reserves one bulletin board for displaying student work, and as the year goes on, he also finds it helpful to post anchor charts that reinforce classroom procedures and routines and academic skills. These can include steps for using the printer, the homeroom morning routine, a monthly calendar with academic and social events, a daily homework log, steps for the homeroom closing routine, and how-to's for various academic skills taught throughout the year.

Positive Teacher Language

According to research, teachers have the ability to influence students' performance in school—both positively and negatively—with the expectations and beliefs we express about them. If we tell and show them that we believe in their ability to achieve success in their academic work, their likelihood of doing so increases. And if we express negative beliefs about their abilities, they are less likely to succeed. This is as true for students' behavior as it is for their academic performance.

Teacher language is one of our most essential and powerful tools for communicating our expectations to students. Effective teacher language can communicate to students both our confidence in their ability to meet high expectations and our recognition of their efforts at behaving well. Our language can also help students visualize positive outcomes for themselves, recognize the beneficial results of their efforts, and get back on task when they make mistakes. It is critical to understand how to use this powerful tool in a purposeful and positive way.

The goal of positive teacher language is to encourage a community built on positive interactions, responsibility, accountability, and trust. In pursuit of that aim, positive teacher language:

- Is clear, simple, and direct

- Is genuine and respectful

- Gives specific positive feedback rather than general praise

- Focuses on a student's action or behavior rather than generalizing about their whole person

- Avoids qualitative or personal judgment

- Shows faith in students' ability to follow the rules

> Teacher language is one of our most essential and powerful tools for communicating our expectations to students.

Envisioning Language

This type of language offers students a chance to picture a goal, imagine how they can achieve it, and believe in their own ability to do so. When teachers use envisioning language to name positive identities for students, those students begin to see themselves as capable learners and problem-solvers. Envisioning language can be posed either as a statement to convey what we believe students are able to achieve, or as a question to invite them into the conversation.

To use envisioning language effectively:

- **Think about positive identities you can apply to the students you teach.** Referring to students as "researchers," "writers," "scientists," "athletes," "teammates," "artists," or "musicians" can generate excitement and help them identify with and inhabit those roles. If you use terms that are new to students—for example, those related to a specific unit of study—make sure they understand what those terms mean to ensure that your envisioning language has the desired effect.

- **Use concrete words and images that students understand.** Rather than putting things in abstract terms ("I know you'll be well-behaved during today's presentations"), try to be specific ("Today's presentations will offer a great opportunity to practice the active listening skills you worked on last week. I look forward to hearing the insightful questions you come up with!"). This can help students form a personal vision of themselves as successful learners.

- **Add clarity and power and increase students' excitement with metaphors.** These metaphors can come from the curriculum, classroom life, or your own experiences. If you are studying Lewis and Clark, for example, you might say, "Today we will continue on our own expedition to discover what happened during Lewis and Clark's journey across the United States."

Reinforcing Language

By reinforcing the things we see students doing well, we help them solidify these behaviors and build on them for ongoing academic and behavioral success. It can be useful to follow up our reinforcements with open-ended questions that allow students to reflect on how they achieved success so that they can do it again next time.

To use reinforcing language effectively:

Examples of Reinforcing Language

"I noticed that you double-checked your work and then corrected your verb conjugation. That attention to detail will help you in all areas of study."

"I'm seeing partners remind each other about how to handle the microscope slides."

"You expressed your opinion politely, even though you and your partner disagreed. What helped you do that?

- **Name concrete, specific behaviors and emphasize description over personal approval.** For example, "You included so many visual details in your poem that I could vividly picture the scene" is more effective than "I really liked your poem." Being specific helps students understand exactly what they're doing well so they can build on it, and keeping the focus on the work rather than on the teacher's opinion helps students learn to assess their own efforts. It also helps them develop their internal sense of self-worth rather than looking to the teacher for validation.

- **Use it authentically with all students.** In every academic area, success will come more easily to some students than to others. But all students deserve to be recognized for their efforts. No matter the end result of a student's efforts, point out what you see them doing well along the way. In order to

IN THE CLASSROOM

Mrs. Wylie

Changing the way we talk can be challenging. When Mrs. Wylie was working on changing her teacher language, she kept a teacher language book handy to reference and posted sticky notes with teacher language she wanted to use on her desk. She also recorded herself during class to track her speech patterns. The results surprised her and informed further changes she wanted to make. Mrs. Wylie believes this culture shift is the responsibility of adults who work with students—we can't change things we don't recognize we are doing.

find positives to name in all students, observe each student carefully and acknowledge the small but important steps they take toward mastery of a skill or behavior.

- **Keep reinforcements private unless they apply to the entire group.** When an individual student does something you want to reinforce, keep your comments discreet. Publicly using one student's behavior as an example for others can cause the individual student to feel manipulated or distrustful of your positive feedback, while their classmates may feel resentful of the student being praised. However, you can direct reinforcing language at a group or the entire class if the whole group is displaying a positive behavior (for example, "I see students transitioning smoothly from partner brainstorming to their study groups").

- **Keep it sincere.** It may take a while to feel natural using this type of language. But students can tell when you are coming from a genuine place. The more intentional practice you put in, the more natural it will feel to use reinforcing language.

Reminding Language

Many of us use reminders to help us or others around us remember to do things like paying a bill or picking up something at the grocery store. Reminding language has a similar purpose—to help students remember what they're supposed to do—but it differs in an important way. Unlike the reminders we adults give ourselves, reminding language doesn't explicitly tell a student what to do but rather prompts them to remember established expectations themselves. By placing the responsibility for remembering what to do on the student, we help them develop a deeper understanding of the rules and how to follow them, and a stronger sense of motivation to do so. This reminding can be posed as a question ("What will it look like to enter the room respectfully?") or a statement ("Show me how to enter the room respectfully"), and may be used to help students remember expectations in preparation for an activity or event, or to help them get back on task when behavior is just beginning to veer off course.

To use reminding language effectively:

- **Establish expectations first.** For reminding language to be effective, students need to have a clear understanding of what the expectations are, so it's essential to teach and practice the procedures and behavior expectations to which the reminders refer.

- **Deliver reminding language with a direct tone and neutral body language.** Our nonverbal communication conveys a lot to students, so it's important that our tone and body language match our words in order to communicate our faith in students' good intentions. One trick for keeping your tone neutral is to visualize the student doing the right thing before you speak. That way, you can offer reminders with the expectation that the student will succeed, which helps keep irritation and judgmental undertones out of your voice.

- **Keep reminders simple and brief.** Long explanations shouldn't be necessary if behavior expectations are clear. In addition, using too many words can make a student feel reprimanded rather than supported, in which case they may tune you out or grow defiant.

- **Use reminding language when the off-task behavior is just beginning.** Pay attention to any signs that students are losing focus or are on the verge of misbehavior. This is when reminders are most effective. If you wait until after a student's annoyed tone in a small group discussion turns into a loud argument, it will be much more difficult for students to rein their behavior back in.

Examples of Reminding Language

A student begins to doodle instead of working on math problems: "What might help you regain focus on this assignment?"

Two students discussing how to complete a collage are starting to raise their voices: "Show me how to express your opinions in a way that follows the rule 'Be kind.'"

Before a whole-school assembly: "What are some ways to follow the rule 'Respect yourself and others' during today's assembly?"

IN THE CLASSROOM

Mrs. Wylie

While the vast majority of misbehaviors in Mrs. Wylie's classroom disappeared once she committed to proactively dealing with them, the issues that do still arise are handled with reminding and redirecting language. Simple questions such as "What are our expectations?" or "What should this activity look like?" help students remember what to do to get back on task.

Redirecting Language

When a student has lost control and their behavior needs to be stopped immediately, redirecting language tells them clearly and directly what to do. Unlike reminding language, which is only appropriate when a student is still calm enough to think through their own behavior, redirecting language lets the teacher take over to get things back on task. This type of language is useful when a student has lost their temper, they aren't paying attention to what they're doing, or there is an immediate safety concern. Redirecting language is nonnegotiable, always given as a statement rather than a question, and it tells the student exactly what to do next so that they can regain control and positive behavior can be restored.

To use redirecting language effectively:

- **Be firm and clear.** Although we may worry about sounding mean when giving redirections, it is possible to be both firm and kind. Not being explicit in our expectations can confuse students, cause them to grow uncertain about limits, and cost us our authority. If you mean "no," then say "no." By being clear and specific, we let students know they can trust us and take us at our word.

- **Use direct statements.** Trying to soften the message by phrasing it as a question may be tempting, but doing so doesn't help students who are having trouble controlling their behavior. And help is exactly what redirecting language offers. Bearing this in mind can keep us on the right track for using redirecting language effectively. Being asked a question gives the student additional cognitive work to do at a time they aren't in a good frame of mind to do it, and can also make your request seem optional. Thus, "Could you please put the scissors down?" does not work as well as simply saying, "Put the scissors down."

- **Consider your tone and volume.** As with redirecting language, keep your tone of voice and body language calm and neutral. Giving redirections as quietly and discreetly as possible helps students maintain their dignity, which makes them more likely to follow the redirection and less likely to grow defiant or frustrated. Unless a redirection applies to the whole group, try to keep it private.

- **Keep it brief and simple.** A long lecture won't help students get back in control of their behavior, and it isn't necessary to get the point across. A quick statement such as "Hands to yourself" or "Pause; pick up your materials" is all that's needed.

It takes time and effort to change our language patterns. The first step is to take a clear look at where you are now. As you speak to students, listen to the words and tone you're using, and think about what your body language conveys. You may want to collaborate with a member of your teaching team or another colleague to give each other feedback and discuss ways to improve your teacher language. Try observing each other and sharing notes afterward on what you saw and heard. You might also video- or audio-record yourself to review your use of language and get a clearer picture of how you come across to students.

After you've assessed your use of teacher language, think about one area where you can start improving. Maybe you've discovered that you frequently cross your arms or let frustration slip into your voice when you're handling misbehavior. Or maybe you've realized you want to use more envisioning language at the beginning of each class or each new unit of study. Start with small changes and work your way up to larger ones. Pausing before you react to students can give you time to think so that you can have better control over your words and tone. If you do make a mistake, show students that you're capable of acknowledging and correcting it: "Pause, rewind. What I meant to say was . . ." Make notes to yourself in your planner about the changes you want to make, set reminders to pop up on your phone, or put a sticky note with words you want to use more frequently on the back of your ID badge.

No matter what changes you strive to make or how you support yourself making them, remember to be patient with yourself. Just as students need to practice new skills in order to grow comfortable with them, we need time and practice to improve our teacher language. Give yourself credit for the small improvements you make along the way.

 To learn more about using positive teacher language, see *The Power of Our Words for Middle School: Teacher Language That Helps Students Learn* (Center for Responsive Schools, 2016).

Teaching and Modeling Procedures and Routines

In order for students to rise to our expectations, they need to know what those expectations look like in action. We can't assume that students already know how to do things the way we want them to. Some may need additional support in certain procedures. Plus, a particular procedure may look different in each classroom. For example, a student may discover that although their sixth grade math teacher wanted them to put their homework in the assigned drop-off spot immediately upon entering the room, their seventh grade math teacher wants them to first take their seat and answer a "Question of the Day" that's written on the board. Thus, we must explicitly teach students the procedures and routines they need to be successful in our classroom.

Interactive Modeling

Interactive Modeling is an effective technique for teaching procedures and routines that need to be done one specific way. Straightforward and direct, Interactive Modeling works by allowing students to observe, think about, discuss, and practice a new skill in order to learn what it looks like, sounds like, and feels like. Instead of simply telling students what to do, Interactive Modeling shows them exactly how to meet expectations. This technique can be used for teaching proce-

◼ IN THE CLASSROOM

Mr. Abdus-Salaam
To make transitions throughout the day go smoothly, Mr. Abdus-Salaam teaches his class how to line up, leave the classroom without disrupting other classes, and change to a new activity. He teaches students a hand signal he uses for quiet, which students can imitate when they see him do it as a way to help their classmates. He also teaches a series of hand signals students can use when they need to make a quick request, such as to use the pencil sharpener. In turn, he uses hand signals to say yes or no, depending on whether it is an appropriate time. By taking responsibility for their needs without interrupting the class's learning, students practice autonomy through the use of these hand signals.

Mr. Moral
On the first day of school, Mr. Moral models basic classroom procedures and routines for students, such as how to respond to his signal for quiet, how to walk in the hallway, how to carry chairs and form a circle in the meeting space, and how to pack up at the end of the period. He also models academic procedures students will need. Mr. Moral collaborates with his teaching team so that each student has a binder with a section

dures (such as how and where to hand in homework assignments), routines (such as what to do when first entering the classroom each day), and academic and social skills (such as engaging with a text or giving and accepting feedback).

The four steps of Interactive Modeling are as follows:

1 **Describe what you will model and why.** This first step is important because it helps students understand the purpose behind what is being modeled. Knowing why they are learning and practicing something increases students' motivation to properly execute the procedure being taught. This is especially true for young adolescents, who are inclined to test limits but are also capable of self-awareness, insight, and empathy. Some students may ask, "Why do we have to learn this?" but will often accept a thoughtful and genuine response.

Once you decide on a procedure to model, it can be helpful to plan ahead of time exactly what you'll say. Keeping your description short will ensure that the actual modeling isn't overshadowed by explanation. Use positive language, even if what you're modeling is in response to a problem, and connect the purpose to the classroom rules. For example, if students have been putting supplies away in a sloppy manner, you might say, "I'm going to show you how to put the supplies away in an organized way so that everyone can easily find what they need. That's going to help you follow our rule 'Respect our school environment.'"

for each class and a place to record short-term and long-term assignments. He and the other teachers on his team take time to teach and model how to organize this binder at the beginning of the school year, and each day, Mr. Moral makes time for students to copy down assignments.

Mrs. Wylie

Mrs. Wylie makes a list of everything she can think of that could be a barrier to learning, and then considers which of those things she can create a routine to help manage. For example, she makes a list of supplies students will need and ensures

that they are accessible in her classroom. She then introduces a routine: one student from each four-person table cluster will be in charge of getting supplies from the bins. Mrs. Wylie then uses Interactive Modeling to teach students the procedure for getting supplies. Modeling this procedure for the whole class helps all students be ready to take on this responsibility if cluster groups change and a new person is chosen to get the supplies, or if the designated person is out for the day and someone else needs to fill in for them.

2 **Model while students notice.** In this step, you demonstrate the actual procedure. This gives students a clear mental image of what's expected of them and how to do it. Modeling is most effective if you practice it beforehand to ensure that you are covering every step you want students to observe and that your modeling is succinct enough to keep students' attention.

Unless talking is part of what you are modeling, it is best to stay silent. Avoid narrating your actions so that students can do the work of noticing for themselves what is important about the procedure. In some cases, it is necessary to make your thinking "visible" for students, such as when modeling how to solve a math problem or edit a paragraph of an essay. In these instances, the think-aloud technique can show students your thought process. For example, when modeling how to refocus one's attention, you could say, "I'm having trouble focusing, so I'm going to take three deep breaths then return to the book I'm reading." You might choose to use a particular signal so that students will know when you're doing a think-aloud, such as putting your hand on your head. Or, you can simply say that you'll be doing a think-aloud to model a certain procedure.

3 **Give students the opportunity to collaborate and practice.** Next, give students the chance to discuss and practice what they just saw you doing. This step is invaluable because not only do students get a chance to ask questions to clarify any confusion, but they are also able to cement the new skill they've observed through intentional practice. By putting what they observed into their own words and then repeating what they saw modeled, students take ownership of the procedure.

Use open-ended questions to help students describe what they saw you doing in their own words: "What did you notice?" "How was I doing it?" It can be helpful to have students discuss what they saw with a partner or in a small group first, and then invite volunteers to share what they discussed. Guide the whole-class conversation as needed to make sure students cover all of the essential elements of the procedure. If a student frames an answer in the negative, such as "You didn't slam the door when you came into the room," ask a follow-up question ("What did I do?") to help them reframe their answer in the positive: "You closed the door gently."

When it comes time for students to practice the procedure, be clear that students should repeat exactly what they saw modeled. Give them the opportunity to once again work with a partner or small group, taking turns as needed and helping one another remember what to do.

4 **Reinforce their practice with immediate feedback.** While students practice, reinforce their efforts. When you notice students successfully practicing what you modeled, specifically name their positive actions: "I'm noticing students check to make sure they are on the right date in their daily planner." When guiding students who are getting off task, do so respectfully but clearly in order to preserve their dignity while helping them find success: "Ferdinand, where does your planner go once you are done writing down your assignments?" Being able to practice in a safe environment is essential for young adolescents, who can be self-conscious and prone to embarrassment.

At the end of practice, invite students to reflect on how they're doing. You might ask, "After practicing that procedure, what is one step you think might be challenging to remember?" or "How will following this procedure each class help you follow our rule 'Take responsibility for your learning'?" Allow them to discuss these questions with a partner or small group to solidify their learning.

Example of Interactive Modeling: Recording Homework Assignments

1. Describe what you will model and why. "Today, I'm going to show you how to record homework assignments for this class. That's going to help you stay organized and follow our guideline 'Be responsible for your own learning.'"

2. Model while students notice. As students watch, take out your daily planner and turn to the date when the homework is due. Locate the assignment on the board, perhaps by pointing to it or walking over and looking at it. Write down the assignment—perhaps looking back at the board several times to indicate that you're writing it exactly as it appears on the board—and then put the daily planner in your bag.

3. Give students the opportunity to collaborate and practice. "Now, you're going to have a few minutes to talk with your table group. What did you notice me doing?" After a few minutes, ask volunteers to share what their groups discussed. Ask questions to help students fill in any missing pieces: "What did I do with my planner after I finished writing down the assignment?" Give students the opportunity to practice by writing down today's homework assignment.

4. Reinforce their practice with immediate feedback. Walk around the room as students practice and point out what you see. "I see students carefully writing down the assignment exactly as it's shown on the board." Discreetly offer any reminders that are needed: "Tara, what's the due date for this assignment?"

After you've taught students a procedure through Interactive Modeling, you may need to occasionally reteach part or all of that procedure as the year goes on. You can set students up for success by giving them proactive reminders before starting an activity: "Take a minute to discuss with a partner how you'll make sure you're walking respectfully in the hallway when we go to the library." You may also find that students need some additional practice in a given procedure. For example, if students need a refresher on how to transition from independent work to group work, you can have them practice while you reinforce their efforts with feedback.

In other cases, such as after a school vacation, you may need to repeat the entire Interactive Modeling process. Remind students that everyone sometimes needs to learn things a few times in order to do them correctly, and frame the repeated Interactive Modeling in a positive way so that students understand your intentions: "I hope everyone had a relaxing vacation! To warm up as we head into the new quarter, let's go back over our routine for starting the day."

The Teacher as Constant Modeler

No matter what grade we teach, we as teachers are always modeling behavior for students, whether by keeping our classrooms neat and organized, speaking respectfully to colleagues, or actively listening when a student is speaking. Young adolescents are starting to form their adult identities and need strong role models as they shape their behavior and personalities. This is why it's so important that we be mindful about the kind of role model we are being for the students we teach.

It isn't always easy to be on our best behavior. How many of us have caught ourselves yelling "Keep your voice down!" or speaking to students in a sarcastic or dismissive way? We all get frustrated, angry, stressed, or tired sometimes, and despite our best efforts, our interactions will not always be ideal. But we can take responsibility for our mistakes, and this in itself is one of the most important skills we can demonstrate for students. Do your best to follow the school or classroom rules, and acknowledge any mistakes you make. By genuinely apologizing and showing students that you're making an effort to do better, you demonstrate that it's possible for them to do the same: "I'm sorry I yelled earlier when I was handing back assignments. I was feeling frustrated and I didn't follow our rule 'Be respectful.'" Saying something like this lets students know that you, too, are doing your best to follow the rules, and that everyone makes mistakes sometimes. It reinforces that nobody's perfect, and that mistakes are a natural part of learning.

Role-Playing

Another way to help students understand what to do and how is through role-playing. Whereas Interactive Modeling teaches how to follow a procedure that needs to be done in one particular way, role-playing is used when there are a variety of positive ways to handle a situation. For example, role-playing might be used to help students practice ways to respectfully disagree during a small group discussion or start a conversation with a peer they don't know well. Role-playing allows students to practice making responsible choices in situations that are more complicated or challenging, particularly social situations. Young adolescents are growing in their ability to think abstractly, plan, and empathize, and role-playing offers a way to build these skills while guiding good behavior in school.

Role-playing can be used in anticipation of an upcoming event, such as a field trip or class project. It can also be used reactively after a one-time or ongoing situation in which the class has had trouble following the rules. For example, if you've instructed students to find a new partner to work with during each class session but they keep gravitating to the same partners, you might use role-playing to help them explore ways to approach and get to know new partners.

The steps of the role-playing process are as follows:

1 **Describe the scenario.** Start out by describing the situation to students in a way that brings it to life. Draw from the life of the classroom to create a realistic scenario, but if the role-play is in response to a particular problem or issue, use hypothetical situations and characters rather than actual events to avoid putting anyone on the spot. For example, if students have been having trouble sticking to an assignment when they reach an obstacle, you might say, "Imagine it's time for writing workshop, and someone goes to their group and says they're stuck. They were able to write their intro paragraph, but now they're not sure how to proceed, and they're starting to feel really frustrated."

2 **Name the goal (but not how to reach it).** Without specifying how to get there, tell students what the desired end result is. Connect this result to the classroom rules and expectations. For example: "The goal is for the student to find a way to get unstuck and move forward with the essay. That's going to let them follow our rule 'Take care of your own learning.'"

3 **Brainstorm ideas and choose one to act out.** Ask students for some ideas about how the student in the scenario might move forward with their essay. Take a few minutes for brainstorming and listing students' ideas. Then, select one idea to act out. Early in the year, it's best if the teacher does this; later on, you might have the class vote on which idea to try first. "We've got five different ideas here. Let's try this one: 'Take a minute to calm down, then ask your writing group for ideas.'"

4 **Act out the idea.** You should take the more active or "tricky" role in the scenario. In this situation, you'd play the role of the frustrated student and ask for volunteers to play the other people in the writing workshop. Take a few minutes to act out the scenario, saying to the pretend workshop group, "I'm so frustrated! I don't know what to do next." Take a moment to take a few deep breaths, then say, "Could you please help me? Maybe you could look at what I have so far and we can talk about what I could write next." After the scenario ends, ask students what they noticed. Then, give students a chance to role-play in small groups, having students take the "tricky" role this time. You might also have them act out some of the other ideas the class brainstormed to let them see alternate ways of handling the situation.

5 **Sum up the learning and follow up.** Reiterate what students said they noticed when they reflected on what they saw in the role-plays. "People noticed that all of these ideas started out with the person calming down. A lot of the ideas you tried also talked about going back over the beginning of the essay or the outline, either by yourself or with your writing group. Think about what might work best for you if you get stuck." As situations similar to the one role-played come up in classroom life, check in with individual students: "Think back on some of the strategies we role-played. What might help you right now to get unstuck?"

Procedures and Skills to Teach at the Beginning of the Year

The first days of the school year can feel a bit overwhelming to both students and teachers, so it's best to prioritize which procedures and skills you most need to teach in the early days of the school year. These essential skills may include:

1 How to use equipment safely

2 Academic skills that will be needed during the first lessons of the year

3 What to do during transition times

4 How to communicate with others to aid in collaborative work and building community

5 How to welcome a new student to the class after the year has begun

The materials that will be used and the skills that will be needed in your classroom will depend on the subjects and topics you teach. It may be helpful to coordinate with your teaching team on procedures that will be common to multiple classrooms, such as handing in homework or requesting a hall pass. Being consistent in how you want students to perform these procedures can help them better meet expectations. For the other types of procedures noted above, the following tips may be useful.

Transition Times

One challenge middle school students face is the increasing number of transitions throughout the day, such as changing classrooms, autonomously switching between activities during class, using lockers between classes, and going to lunch or activities on their own. Establishing expectations for these times is a critical way to help students feel safe and supported and to promote a healthy and respectful school community.

Early in the school year, be sure to teach the procedures students need to know for transition times. These procedures might include:

- Entering the classroom

- Requesting a pass for a bathroom break

- Preparing for dismissal

- Walking through the hallway between classes

- Using lockers appropriately

- Entering and leaving shared school spaces such as the cafeteria, gymnasium, or auditorium

- Waiting for the bus

■ IN THE CLASSROOM

Mr. Abdus-Salaam

Mr. Abdus-Salaam institutes routines for the beginning and end of each class period. Because he knows middle school students tend to come into class talking, he has his homeroom line up in front of the classroom, then reinforces expectations for the day, including a reminder for students to head into the classroom with their voices "on zero." He follows up by saying "Thumbs up if you understand" to make sure everyone is ready. Mr. Abdus-Salaam also records his expectations on the board for students to reference. For example: "Take your chair down from your desk, then come meet in morning circle." Five minutes before the end of class, he once again has students line up. This routine helps them get into a calm mindset before they enter the hallway, go to their lockers, and head to their next class.

Early on, Mr. Abdus-Salaam invests his class in these routines by discussing the reasons behind them and by asking open-ended questions, such as: "How does being quiet in the hall help you live by the rules?" Reflecting on these questions allows his class to understand how their behavior in the hallway affects both them and other students in the school.

In order to extend these expectations into transitional spaces that are shared by all members of the school community, reinforce them as students begin a new class period and as they are getting ready to leave your classroom. As with all expectations, use teacher language to support students as they learn expectations, and model specific routines and procedures again as necessary.

Of course, even after proactively setting expectations for transitions, missteps are bound to occur. Use these as teachable moments. Just as you would in your classroom, verbally reinforce the positive behavior you are seeing, while redirecting students who are getting off task. At times when a student requires more support than a simple verbal reminder, remember to maintain their dignity by talking with them privately and respectfully rather than calling them out in front of their peers.

Mrs. Wylie

Mrs. Wylie relies on hand signals paired with a chime to communicate every transition in her classroom, from starting a new activity to preparing to leave for the next class period. Rather than raising her voice, she prefers this hand signal and chime combination because it is calmer and more neutral. This is especially important for students who may be experiencing toxic stress, to whom a raised voice may sound like anger and trigger a stress response. (See Chapter 5 to learn more about supporting students who are experiencing toxic stress.)

Mr. Moral

Mr. Moral bookends his class periods with routines to help students transition into and out of his classroom. At the start of a class period, he posts a "Do Now" message with tasks that have been taught through Interactive Modeling. A visual timer lets students know how long they have to complete these tasks, allowing students to confidently and immediately get started on their work. Toward the end of the class period, Mr. Moral again uses a visual timer to let students know it's time to wrap up what they are working on. Then, he closes the lesson by having students put their thumb up or down to show whether they understand the content or have completed an assignment, having students hand in their assignment, or designating some other signal to transition students out of their seats and into the hallway.

Communication Skills

Especially at the beginning of the year, when students are getting used to new classes, teachers, and peers, they need instruction in and reinforcement of communication skills. Helpful skills to teach at the beginning of the year may include:

- How to introduce yourself

- How to ask someone their name if you don't remember it

- How to start a conversation with someone you don't know well

- How to ask someone to join your group if they're by themselves

In addition to teaching these skills, you can support students by posting anchor charts or other visuals with reminders, such as a list of conversation starters or techniques they can use to remember people's names.

■ IN THE CLASSROOM

Mr. Abdus-Salaam

Using the *Responsive Classroom* practice of Responsive Advisory Meeting helps new students acclimate to Mr. Abdus-Salaam's classroom in a low-risk way. Students get an opportunity to greet each other, share interests, and learn more about their peers. During the activity portion of the meeting, students develop camaraderie by working together to accomplish a task. Mr. Abdus-Salaam also has current class members help out a new student. These helpers eat lunch with the new student, help them get all their materials organized, and answer questions the new student has. This task is so popular in his classroom that Mr. Abdus-Salaam has to randomly select craft sticks with students' names on them to determine who gets to be a helper.

Mrs. Wylie

Because her classroom often sees as many as three new students a month, Mrs. Wylie has a definitive plan for helping them get acclimated. First, she arranges to meet with them during lunch or at some other convenient time. At the meeting, she teaches the new student the most important routines, including the "4 Gs" students follow when they enter her classroom:

When a New Student Joins the Class

Consider having a conversation with the class at the beginning of the school year to prepare them for the possibility of new students coming in, and to enlist the class in welcoming newcomers. Have students think about what would make them feel welcomed if they were new and brainstorm ideas for things they could do to support a new classmate. Ask for volunteers who would be willing to act as helpers and show new students around, eat lunch with them, and help them navigate schedules and transitions. Sharing this responsibility among multiple students keeps it from falling exclusively on any one person and also helps the new student develop connections with a wider range of classmates.

Keep a spare set of books and required materials on hand so that any new student will be able to immediately participate in class. It's also useful to prepare a few activities to help new students acclimate to the class. These icebreakers might be similar to ones you use at the beginning of a new school year or semester to help all students get to know each other. For example, you might have current students introduce themselves and share a fact about themselves (their favorite subject, their favorite food, or something that makes them unique) and allow the new student to do the same. Before doing any of this, take a moment to privately welcome the new student to the class and gauge whether they seem like they would be open to such activities rather than feeling put on the spot. Whether or not you choose to do any icebreaker activities, the arrival of a new student is one of many good times to have a refresher conversation about the rules, expectations, and procedures for the class. Doing so not only helps the new student but serves as a helpful reminder to all students in the class.

greet Mrs. Wylie, go read the daily message, get their supplies, and get to work. Because her school has a large population of English language learners, Mrs. Wylie has pictures of each routine available. Once she has taught these routines, she and the new student practice them. Being able to confidently participate in established class routines allows new students to more easily adjust to their new environment.

Mr. Moral
Prior to a new student's first day in his classroom, Mr. Moral tries to meet with both the student and their parents. This gives the student a chance to begin getting to know him and learning about the classroom routines and schedules. He also keeps a folder labeled "New Student" in which he places important handouts, such as the class supply list and packets for each unit of study. In addition, he keeps a set of basic supplies handy in case a new student arrives unexpectedly. Mr. Moral designates a helper or two to support the student throughout the first school day with transitions and routines, and he uses this opportunity to quickly review expectations of important routines and procedures with all students.

Building a Foundation for Learning

1 Prepare students for success by organizing the classroom in a way that allows students to retrieve materials and information easily and collaborate successfully.

2 Use positive teacher language that envisions successful outcomes for students, reinforces what they're doing well, reminds them to follow classroom procedures and routines, and redirects them when they don't follow the rules.

3 Use Interactive Modeling and role-playing to teach and allow practice of essential procedures, routines, and skills.

7-2's TEAM EXPECTATIONS

1. Respect the chime all the time.

2. C.A.R.E.S.
   self Control
   Empathy
   Assertion
   Responsibility
   coOperation

3. Never settle for less than your best.

4. Be prompt & prepared.

5. Treat others the way you want to be treated.

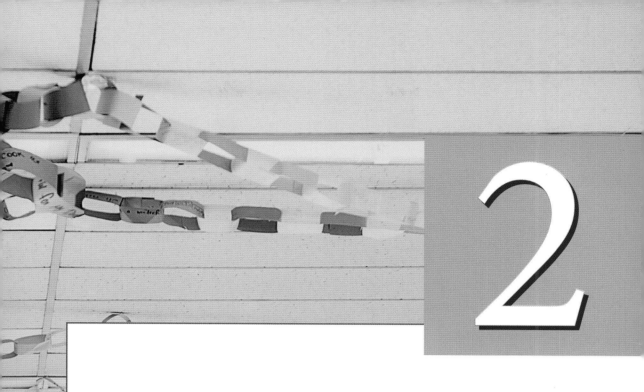

Working With the Rules

Working With the Rules

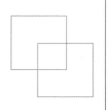

The *Responsive Classroom* approach to discipline puts a great deal of emphasis on proactive techniques like those described in Chapter 1. Investing time and effort in laying a strong foundation and teaching students what the expectations are and how to follow them will greatly reduce the amount of time spent responding to misbehavior.

The work of proactive discipline continues with the practices in this chapter, which focus on helping students set achievable and meaningful goals for themselves, and instilling the belief in students that the rules can help them meet those goals. These practices help students understand the value in following the rules and develop the intrinsic motivation to do so.

Having clear guidelines for behavior can have many benefits. School or classroom rules can help:

- Create a comforting sense of order and predictability, which allows students to feel safer and participate more fully

- Foster a healthy school climate where interactions are kind and respectful

- Guide students to develop and strengthen self-control

- Promote social awareness and a sense of responsibility

- Balance the individual's needs with the group's needs

Whether students wish to become stronger in an academic subject, take on a leadership role in student government, make more friends, or improve their study skills, the rules can help them find success.

Guidance on Establishing Rules

In some schools, there is a list of schoolwide rules that all students are expected to follow. In others, teachers create their own classroom or team rules. If you're involved in creating rules for your school or classroom, consider the following guidelines for coming up with a positive and constructive list of rules for students to live by.

Effective rules work by framing ideals and presenting them as positive statements, such as "Be kind," "Take care of school resources," or "Respect yourself and others." The goal is to guide students to reflect on what positive behavior looks like rather than simply telling them what to do—or what not to do. Presenting the rules in a global manner promotes this kind of reasoned, critical, and ethical thinking. Rules stated this way can be applied to the wide variety of scenarios that may arise in school, so they encourage deeper understanding by allowing students to think through how to apply them.

Three to five rules are enough to cover just about every situation while still being easy for students to remember. Consider a list including rules that touch on these categories:

- Taking care of and respecting oneself
- Taking care of and respecting others
- Taking care of and respecting school spaces and materials
- Doing one's best work

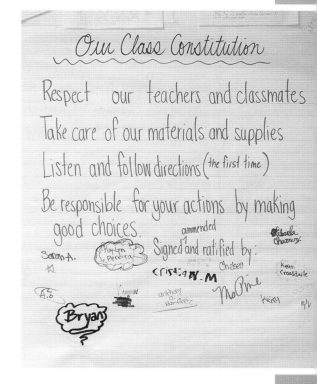

If you are part of a teaching team, discuss with your teammates how you expect the rules to look when they're in action in your classrooms. Having consistency among classes can help students feel confident in knowing how they're expected to behave and how the rules will be enforced.

Investing Students in the Rules

As students practice essential skills and procedures and grow more comfortable with the basic routines of the classroom, with you, and with each other, they're ready to become invested in the classroom rules. The process of investing students in the rules has four steps:

- Set SMART goals

- Connect goals to the rules so students understand how the rules are designed to support them and their classmates in reaching those goals

- Show students how the rules connect to concrete behaviors

- Make the rules come alive by referring to them regularly and making them visible in the classroom

It may be helpful to spread this process over multiple days to allow time for students to reflect on each step.

Helping Students Overcome Self-Consciousness During the Goal-Setting Process

Middle school students are prone to self-consciousness, and fear of their peers' judgment can cause some to become defensive. This can result in their trying to make a joke of the goal-setting process or proposing superficial or unrealistic goals, such as "I want to take a nap every day" or "Putting a roller coaster in the gymnasium."

For this reason, it's beneficial to wait until you've built some trust and affiliation before having students set goals. By then, most students will have decided that it's safe to share their true goals. A respectful audience can help students think and talk about what matters to them in school, so consider using Interactive Modeling to teach students how to respectfully listen to and comment on what others have to say. For any student who is still struggling to take the assignment seriously after that, it may help for you to have a one-on-one conversation with them in which you demonstrate your trustworthiness and show that you respect what they think.

The goals of this collaborative process are to:

- Create a shared vision of expectations and how the learning environment will support everyone's growth

- Make explicit how each rule will look, sound, and feel when being followed

- Build students' understanding of how their actions contribute to their success and to the success of others

Step 1: Setting SMART Goals

The first step of this process is to help students set goals that are personally meaningful to them. These goals are called SMART goals because they are:

S **Specific**—The goal is well defined and focused, and the student understands the benefits of setting it.

M **Measurable**—There is a clear endpoint or amount of progress the student is aiming for.

A **Achievable**—It is realistic for the student to complete this goal with a reasonable amount of effort.

R **Relevant**—The goal will make a positive difference in the student's life and will help them improve their own specific situation.

T **Time-bound**—There is a deadline for achieving the goal.

By having students set their own goals for school, you communicate to them that what they think and feel matters. Goal-setting also encourages students to take responsibility for their own learning because they have a more personal stake in doing so.

To help students start thinking about their goals, guide them to consider what matters to them. One place to begin is to ask students to reflect on some of their accomplishments from last year that they are most proud of, as well as areas where they would like to improve. Another option is to share a class syllabus or overview of what they'll be learning during the quarter, semester, or year to pique their interest and help them think more concretely about specific content and challenges. You could also have them brainstorm career goals or interests and think about the skills they would need to achieve those goals.

SMART goals can be behavioral, academic, or social:

- **Behavioral goals** focus on the behaviors that support students' success in school.

- **Academic goals** help students consider how they'd like to improve or build on their unique abilities and interests, as well as find success with the academic content they'll tackle soon.

- **Social goals** help students connect with their peers, identify supportive friends, and be a good friend to others. Social goals are especially important during early adolescence, when students are exploring their identities as individuals and as members of a group.

Next, have students think about possible behavioral, academic, or social goals for the year ahead or for a shorter time period, such as the first month or quarter, by asking or posting questions to prompt students' thinking. These goals must simply be things they can work on in school. As part of this process, you might try sharing your own goal with the class. This shows them that goal-setting is an important part of successful adult life and demonstrates that your classroom is a safe, respectful space for sharing what matters most to them.

■ IN THE CLASSROOM

Mr. Moral

Near the beginning of the school year, Mr. Moral previews key concepts his class will study to get them excited about the year ahead. For homework that night, students write a short reflection about something that excites them about the upcoming year. The next day, he has students share their reflections with partners and small groups, then poses the question, "What is something that you hope to achieve this year?" Students share their responses with a partner. After some time for discussion, Mr. Moral moves students into goal-setting by asking them to identify one academic and one social goal for the upcoming school year. He advises students to choose goals

they are comfortable sharing publicly since they will be posted on the bulletin board. Students write these during the first week of school, and by the end of the first week, all goals are on display for classmates to see and support.

Mrs. Wylie

Mrs. Wylie shares her own goal as a teacher with her classes. By sharing a goal she really wants to accomplish during the school year and why she considers it important, she shows students that setting goals and working toward them is a lifelong habit. This helps frame goal-setting as personally meaningful for the students rather than something they have to do to make the teacher happy.

Once students have brainstormed a list of possible goals, it's time for them to choose a single SMART goal for your class. They should evaluate the potential goal to see if it fits all five criteria of a SMART goal, and adjust it if necessary.

- **Specific**—The goal is well-defined and focused, and the student can articulate both why the goal is important and how they will benefit from achieving it. To help students refine an ambiguous or incomplete goal, have them consider the following questions: Can I describe what I want to accomplish in one phrase or sentence? Is my goal focused on one specific achievement? Can I explain the reasons why I want to accomplish it? Can I explain the specific benefits of accomplishing this goal?

- **Measurable**—How will the student measure their progress? Pose questions such as the following: Is there an external measure of success, such as a grade? How am I now and how will I be different? What things will I be able to do that I'm not able to do now? How are my relationships now and how will they be different?

- **Achievable**—An achievable goal is one that is realistic for a student to accomplish with a reasonable amount of effort in the time allotted. Students should consider which factors are in their control; for example, "winning the science fair" is not a realistic goal, since too many factors are outside the student's control, but "completing a project for the science fair" is.

- **Relevant**—Goals are relevant when achieving them is worth the effort because doing so will make a positive difference in the student's life. One way for students to assess this component is by comparing what would happen if they achieved the goal versus what would happen if they didn't. Would they gain or miss out on an opportunity? Would they experience satisfaction or disappointment? How will accomplishing the goal impact their relationships with others? Will not achieving the goal put them at a disadvantage?

- **Time-bound**—There is a target date for achieving the goal and milestones for progress along the way. Have students consider how much time they need to achieve their goal, how much time they have, and what changes they expect to see and when.

Creating SMART Goals

Goals	Sample prompts	Sample SMART goals
Behavioral goals	• What can you do when you get stuck on an assignment? • How can you manage anger or frustration when things are difficult or don't go your way?	• By the end of the semester, I want to learn at least three new strategies to help me find solutions when I get stuck on an assignment. • This quarter, I will learn relaxation techniques to use when I get frustrated, and I will practice them for five minutes each day.
Academic goals	• What do you want to achieve in your classes this semester? • How will you show others what you've learned in a particular unit or class?	• This year, I want to improve my time-management skills by consistently using my planner to track homework, tests, and activities. • I will create a visual display for my end-of-quarter science project.
Social goals	• How can you strengthen your communication skills this year? • What characteristics make someone a good friend?	• This year, I will have lunch with at least one person per month whom I don't know well. • This quarter, I will join the cooking club so that I can meet new people who share my interests.

■ IN THE CLASSROOM

Mr. Abdus-Salaam

To help his students set SMART goals, Mr. Abdus-Salaam starts with the end result and works backward. He asks, "What are you hoping to learn this year?" From there, they discuss the steps needed to accomplish that. Students fill out a new SMART goal planner at the beginning of each grading period. As students track their progress and check off goals they accomplish, they can clearly see the progress they are making, which in turn encourages them to keep going. Mr. Abdus-Salaam further facilitates students' reflection by building debrief time into the schedule so that students can discuss what they did to progress toward their goal. He understands that developmental characteristics play a role in how much support students need—older students tend to thrive given more autonomy to pursue their SMART goals, while younger students need more guidance and can benefit from one-on-one meetings to discuss progress and strategies for moving forward.

By considering and responding to the components of a SMART goal, students are equipped with the information they need to fill out a SMART goal planner, which lets them note their goal, what they have to do to achieve it, the milestones they will look for to see progress, and the target date for achieving the goal.

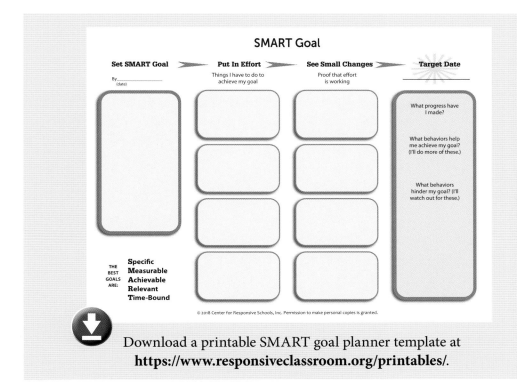

SMART Goal

Set SMART Goal → **Put In Effort** → **See Small Changes** → **Target Date**

By_____
(date)

Things I have to do to achieve my goal

Proof that effort is working

What progress have I made?

What behaviors help me achieve my goal? (I'll do more of these.)

What behaviors hinder my goal? (I'll watch out for these.)

THE BEST GOALS ARE:
Specific
Measurable
Achievable
Relevant
Time-Bound

Download a printable SMART goal planner template at
https://www.responsiveclassroom.org/printables/.

Consider collecting students' SMART goal planners after they're filled out. This will allow you to carefully review the goals and offer any feedback, encouragement, or clarifying questions to help students refine their goals, if needed. It also enables you to record students' goals, perhaps on a page in your planner or in a spreadsheet, so that you can regularly refer to them and support and track students' progress.

When you return students' SMART goal planners to them, take time to discuss how to keep their goals organized for all of their classes. Work with your teaching team to come up with a system that all students on the team can use, such as creating a section at the front of their binder for all of their SMART goal planners and having weekly check-ins during homeroom to assess their progress.

Step 2: Connecting Goals to the Rules

After students have set their goals and mapped out a plan to achieve them, the next step is to help them connect those goals to the rules. This helps students understand the rules as a positive influence that supports them in achieving their goals and creating the kind of community where everyone supports each other.

Have students consider specific ways in which the rules relate to the goals they've set. They can do this through a freewriting activity, quiet reflection, or discussion with a partner or small group. While a student might not immediately see how every rule supports their goal, everyone should be able to connect their goal to at least one rule. When students are ready, ask for a few volunteers to share their connections. Try and find at least one connection for each rule. For example:

- "I want to get at least a B+ in English this quarter. Following the rule 'Do your best work' means I should spend more time on my rough drafts so I can write stronger essays."

- "This semester, I want to make friends with at least two people who like to play the same kind of music I do. If I follow the rule 'Respect others,' it will help me get to know more people and learn about their interests."

- "I want to dissect a frog this year. The rule 'Respect our materials and resources' means I will learn how to use the scalpel safely so I don't accidentally hurt myself or my partner."

When students are done sharing, emphasize to the class that while they may not see how every rule supports their own goal right now, each rule supports someone's goal. This will reinforce that all the rules are important, since they are all tools that support people's goals. The objective here is to frame the rules as positive guidelines that help create the kind of community where everyone works together to help one another succeed. Referring to these guidelines as "our rules" helps reinforce this idea and give students a greater sense of ownership.

IN THE CLASSROOM

Mrs. Wylie
After Mrs. Wylie's students have set goals, they brainstorm what the classroom needs to look, sound, and feel like to reach those goals. Mrs. Wylie then leads a discussion about how the class rules can support the environment that students just described.

Throughout the year, Mrs. Wylie reminds students of how the rules can support their goals by asking questions such as, "Which rule fits best for what we are doing?"

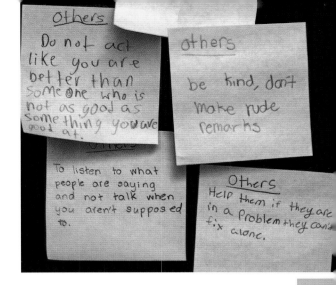

Before moving on to the next step, prime students' thinking about how the rules will look, sound, and feel in action. Have them reflect on what they'll need from others in the class to reach their own goal, and what they can do to help others achieve their goals. These reflections help shape the learning community as a place where everyone's goals matter.

Step 3: Connecting the Rules to Concrete Behavior

Because of the global nature of the rules, students need to think through how the rules will translate to day-to-day activities and behaviors. For this reason, it is important to help students connect the rules to concrete, observable behaviors. Using the goals students have shared and the connections they've made between their goals and the rules, have them work in small groups to brainstorm what it will look, sound, and feel like to follow the rules in support of those goals.

Here are some possible reflection questions you could pose to get the brainstorming started:

- How can you make the classroom a peaceful and calm space where everyone can do their best work?

- How can you follow the rule "Be respectful" during group discussions?

- What are some specific things you could do to help keep the classroom organized so that everyone can focus?

Once the groups are finished brainstorming, ask for volunteers to share some of the ideas that were mentioned. You might choose to record these ideas on an anchor chart to help students remember how the rules will look, sound, and feel in action.

You might also pose specific scenarios and ask students how the rules might apply to each. For example:

- You finish a test early and have some extra time while everyone else continues working.

- One of your tablemates accidentally knocks over some paint and it spills across the table.

- The whole class is headed to an all-school assembly.

In these scenarios, encourage students to find connections that go beyond the obvious. For example, students might say they can "Respect our materials" by having all tablemates pitch in to clean up the spill, but they might also "Respect others" by staying calm and quiet as they do so to allow everyone around them to continue working without getting distracted.

By guiding students to make connections between their goals, the rules, and concrete behaviors, you're helping them understand how they can use the rules in support of their goals for the year, as well as helping them see the significance of their role in creating a positive classroom culture. You are also helping them develop motivation to follow the rules so that they and their classmates can achieve their goals.

■ IN THE CLASSROOM

Mrs. Wylie
Early in the school year, Mrs. Wylie discusses with students how the classroom's four core rules should look and sound in action. For example, the rule "Take care of others" might look like offering encouraging words to a classmate. The answers students come up with go on anchor charts, which Mrs. Wylie laminates and hangs up in the room.

Mr. Moral
Mr. Moral uses the introduction and closing of a lesson to connect rules to concrete behaviors. During the introduction, when the learning goals are being defined, he might ask, "What is one way you can take care of your learning as we discuss text-to-text connections?" A quick conversation like this reminds students of the value of the rules and sets a purpose for the upcoming work. During the closing, he again has the class take a few moments to reflect on the rules. For example, he might ask, "How did you support your science group members in meeting today's learning goal?" or "What is something you might try differently next time to help you work with your group?"

Mr. Moral also connects to the rules when giving directions. For example, if students are about to work on a science investigation in small groups, he might ask, "How can you show you are taking care of your learning and the learning of others during group work today?" Proactive reminders like these help to build a positive community and hold students accountable to the rules. When necessary, he also uses Interactive Modeling or role-playing to connect the rules to specific behaviors and to ensure students understand expectations.

Step 4: Making the Rules Come Alive

The final step of investing students in the rules integrates the rules into the daily life of the classroom. This work begins as part of the initial rule-investment process and continues throughout the year. You can make the rules come alive in your classroom by:

- Posting the rules in a prominent place for students to see and refer to each day

- Referring to the rules frequently in the natural course of teaching

- Revisiting the rules as needed, such as after a holiday break or during a midyear slump, when a new student joins the class, or any time you feel that students could use a refresher

Teacher language can help keep the rules front and center throughout the year. When we reference the rules while using reinforcing language, students can make the connection between the rules and their success: "You went out of your way to help our new student today. That shows you're really getting our rule 'Be kind.'" Similarly, it's helpful to bring up the rules while employing proactive reminding language before a task ("How will you follow the rule 'Respect school resources' as you start work on your pottery projects today?") and reactive reminding language when students are beginning to get off task ("Show me how to follow the rule 'Respect school resources' right now as you use the pottery wheel").

Referring to the rules in your teacher language has the benefit of taking the focus off of yourself and putting it on the rules that have been established as being there to support students' goals. The following chart offers ideas for shifting the focus of your teacher language onto the rules in order to foster self-control and ethical, responsible behavior.

■ IN THE CLASSROOM

Mr. Abdus-Salaam

Mr. Abdus-Salaam conducts a Socratic seminar with his class to discuss the "why" behind each rule. He poses open-ended questions (for example, "What are some ways these rules help us build a stronger school community?"), which students discuss in small groups. This makes students a responsible part of creating the guidelines around discipline and gives them a chance to explain their reasoning. Each group appoints a note-taker and presenter. At the end of the Socratic seminar, the presenter from each group shares their group's thinking. Students get a chance to hear their peers' thoughts on why the rules are important and how they support everyone in doing their best work.

Using Teacher Language That Focuses on the Rules

Instead of a teacher-centered approach…	…use a rules-centered approach
"I expect everyone to be quiet and listen to the speaker during our assembly today."	"What are some specific ways you can follow our class rules during the assembly today?"
"Thank you for cleaning up the water that spilled, James. I really appreciated that."	"James, you cleaned up the water that spilled right away without being asked. That helped keep people from slipping and really respects our rule 'Take care of others.'"
"I liked how neatly everyone organized their materials at the end of the last activity."	"You all did an excellent job following our rule 'Take care of school resources' after the last activity when you put everything away so neatly."
"I'll be watching to see how you all greet our new student today."	"One of our rules is 'Respect others.' How might you follow that rule today when the new student joins the class?"
"I'm getting very frustrated that people aren't focused on doing their research right now."	"Everyone, let's refocus. How can you follow our rule to 'Do your best work' as you do your research?"

After going through the four steps of investing students in the rules, you may also want to plan a short meeting in which students officially sign on that they agree to those rules. This agreement could be verbal or written—for instance, students might sign their names to the list of rules displayed on the classroom wall. Agreeing to the rules does not guarantee that students will always follow them, but it allows students to acknowledge the importance of the rules in creating the kind of community in which everyone can achieve their goals. This meeting can also be a chance to celebrate as a community.

Helping Students Get Back in Control of Their Behavior

At this point, you've implemented a number of proactive strategies for teaching discipline. Students know what the rules are, have connected those rules to their own goals, and understand how the rules will look and sound in a variety of situations. They've also studied and practiced important classroom routines. They're as prepared as possible to follow the rules. Yet, sometimes, behavior will still go off course. Just as with a new academic skill, students need time to practice and opportunities to learn from their mistakes in order to improve.

When a student misbehaves, it is the teacher's role to let them know where the boundaries and limits are. Helping students just as they begin to go off task lets them get back in control before misbehavior escalates. It also helps the class as a whole stay focused on learning and reinforces for both the individual and the class that this is a predictable, consistent, and safe space for learning. The strategies below are useful for helping students get back on course when they are just beginning to stray from the rules. These strategies are also useful early in the year before the process of goal-setting and investing students in the rules has been completed.

> Helping students just as they begin to go off task lets them get back in control before misbehavior escalates.

Teacher Proximity

Sometimes, simply walking over and standing near a student is enough to help them become aware of themselves and adjust their behavior to meet classroom expectations. Such a technique uses silence skillfully, and preserves the dignity of the student by drawing as little attention to them as possible. It also allows you to continue instruction uninterrupted. When using proximity, simply stand close enough to the student that they are aware of your presence. For example, if a student is texting during class, walking over and standing next to them as you continue instruction may be enough to get them to put their phone away. When expectations are clear, a teacher's simple presence can do the talking.

Visual and Verbal Cues

Visual cues—such as eye contact, a head nod, or a hand signal—are another way to remind students to follow expectations. Visual cues can be used to help students practice self-control, such as a simple finger to the lips to indicate it is time to stop talking. Or, you might make eye contact with a student who is whispering to a tablemate. This lets the student know you see what they're doing but allows them to take charge of their own behavior in a way that preserves their dignity.

Verbal cues can be as straightforward as saying the student's name or employing reminding or redirecting language to prompt students to remember expectations. Such cues communicate to the student that you know they know what to do, and you are simply giving them a little encouragement to exercise self-discipline. Both visual and verbal cues are meant to minimize the attention drawn to a student who needs help getting their behavior back under control, a consideration that holds great weight in middle school.

Don't Overuse Cues and Reminders

While these strategies can be effective ways to help students regain control of their behavior, cues and reminders can lose their effect if used too frequently. Students who receive one reminder after another might start tuning these signals out once they realize that they don't need to change their behavior until the third or fourth reminder. If a teacher repeatedly stands in close proximity to a student who's playing a game on the computer instead of doing research, but allows the student to continue using the computer, the power of the reminder is undermined. Remember that these cues and reminders are meant to help students learn self-control and self-regulation, and an overreliance on cues and reminders can have the opposite effect.

IN THE CLASSROOM

Mrs. Wylie
In Mrs. Wylie's classroom, students use hand signals to get her attention without having to disrupt the learning of their classmates. Their hand signal tells her, "I need you to come here." Her signal in response communicates, "I saw you and I'm coming."

Working With the Rules

1　An ideal list of rules is brief and easy to remember, is phrased in the positive, and frames the rules as ideals that can be applied to many different situations.

2　Build motivation to follow the rules by guiding students through the process of setting SMART goals, connecting those goals to the rules, connecting the rules to concrete behavior, and continuing to make the rules come alive throughout the school year.

3　Use visual and verbal cues and increased teacher proximity at the first signs of behavior starting to stray from the rules in order to help students get back on task.

3

Responding
to Misbehavior

Responding to Misbehavior

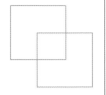

The proactive steps outlined in the first two chapters of this book comprise a large part of the work of discipline, and will help to greatly reduce the amount of time and energy you spend responding to misbehavior. However, there will still be times when students misbehave. They are in the process of learning how to behave appropriately, and mistakes are part of the learning process. Misbehavior is bound to happen to matter how much we plan ahead to prevent it.

This chapter outlines techniques for responding to common misbehaviors, such as chatting with friends at inappropriate times or misusing classroom materials—the sort of everyday lapses that occasionally occur with every student. In this chapter, the focus is on isolated incidents of students not following the rules. How to respond to more chronic or serious behavior issues will be covered in Chapters 4 and 5.

■ IN THE CLASSROOM

Mr. Abdus-Salaam
Mr. Abdus-Salaam believes that misbehavior usually happens either because instructors aren't explicit in their expectations or because students have idle time during a class period and need to be

Why Do Students Misbehave?

How many times in your life have you needed to get the other side of the street and crossed at a place where there was no crosswalk? Although jaywalking is illegal, many people do it anyway. Perhaps we are running late, everyone around us is doing it, we are close enough to a crosswalk and traffic isn't moving anyhow, we are distracted, we are angry or frustrated about something else, or we simply aren't paying that much attention.

Our reasons for jaywalking are generally driven by our own needs and impulses rather than a desire to intentionally disrespect or anger drivers, other pedestrians, or the police or others tasked with enforcing the rules. In the same way, students generally don't misbehave with the goal of frustrating or offending teachers. Like adults, young adolescents have many moments when they give in to their impulses and emotions rather than behaving in a way that aligns with their rational thoughts. Any adult can attest to the fact that it can take a lifetime to learn to behave in a thoughtful, measured way and not give in to one's impulses, and students are still in the early stages of this process. As young adolescents navigate new freedoms and responsibilities, they naturally test limits and are thus likely to make mistakes with their behavior. These mistakes offer rich and vital opportunities for learning.

Just like with an academic subject, students need practice to solidify their learning about positive behavior expectations. The mistakes they make as they progress in that learning are opportunities for us to teach students self-control and responsibility. To do this effectively, we need to practice empathy while still maintaining high standards. That means calmly and firmly enforcing expectations and considering why a student might be misbehaving rather than making assumptions about their character.

engaged. Avoiding either of these scenarios requires planning ahead, both in terms of proactively teaching and modeling expectations and planning engaging, interactive lessons. Mr. Abdus-Salaam also knows that adolescent insecurities can be a factor in student misbehavior. He knows trying to act cool in front of peers can have a domino effect, so incidents of misbehavior must be handled with care so they don't escalate.

Goals in Responding to Misbehavior

An essential goal of responding to misbehavior is to stop negative behavior and reestablish positive behavior so that students can return to learning and the teacher can focus on teaching. Stopping the misbehavior should be done simply and quickly. Doing this shows students that you will respectfully hold firm to the limits and expectations you've set, which helps you maintain an orderly classroom where students can do their best learning.

> As with any new topic or set of skills, students deserve the chance to learn from and correct their mistakes.

Another goal of responding to misbehavior is to help students recognize their misbehavior and replace it with a desired behavior. As with any new topic or set of skills, students deserve the chance to learn from and correct their mistakes. To facilitate that learning, we must go beyond simply telling them what to do. By experiencing relevant, nonpunitive consequences, students develop their own understanding of why it's important to respect school supplies, why it's distracting to a speaker when classmates are chatting amongst themselves, and why it's hurtful to laugh at someone. In the process, students internalize the rules, learn to take responsibility for their actions, and develop self-regulation, skills that are critical to their success both in and out of school.

Finally, remember that it's essential to preserve the dignity of the student and the group. Dealing with misbehavior discreetly can help you avoid causing the student undue embarrassment (which might make them act out even more to try and save face with their peers). Teacher empathy is crucial here—the way we react to a student influences how students react to each other. A response that assumes a student's best intentions and that focuses on the behavior rather than the student's character communicates that this is a learning moment, that it's okay to make mistakes, and that this classroom is a safe place to learn.

Logical Consequences

All students will at some point forget or choose not to follow a rule. Logical consequences are a set of strategies for responding to misbehavior that set clear limits and help students see how their actions affect themselves and others. By making these connections, logical consequences help students develop self-control and internal motivation to do what's right.

Logical consequences differ from punishment in a number of important ways. The message punishment sends to the student is that they are the problem, a message they may internalize, which can have the effect of lowering the student's performance in school. Punishment can have the long-term effect of encouraging students to use evasion and deception to avoid getting in trouble. On the other hand, logical consequences help students keep misbehavior in perspective and understand better what to do next time.

Punishment vs. Logical Consequences

	Punishment	**Logical consequences**
Intention	To ensure compliance by using external controls that make the student feel ashamed or bad in other ways	To help students recognize the effects of their actions and develop internal controls
Underlying belief	Students will do better only because they fear punishment and will seek to avoid it	Students want to do better and can do better with reflection and practice
Teacher's approach and tone	Reacts automatically with little thought; voice is angry and punitive	Gathers more information before reacting; voice is calm and matter-of-fact
Nature of the consequence	Not related to the behavior or the damage done; not reasonable for the student to do	Related to the behavior; reasonable for the student to do
Message to the student	The student is the problem	The damage done, not the student, is the problem

Unlike punishment, logical consequences are:

- **Respectful**—One's word choice, tone of voice, facial expression, and body language should all show respect for the student when giving a logical consequence. A firm and calm tone, quiet volume, and neutral facial expression and body language send the message that you are trying to help the student, not to embarrass them. Focusing your message on the behavior ("Put down the paints and go get some paper towels to clean up the spill") rather than the student's character ("You're such a mess") also lets students know you respect them.

- **Related**—A logical consequence should clearly relate to the misbehavior it's meant to address. For example, if a student is continually whispering to a friend during group work, the student might need to work in a different group for the rest of the class period. Explicitly connecting the consequence to the related classroom rule helps ensure that you are focusing on the rule-breaking behavior rather than directing any judgment at the student's character: "Whispering keeps you from following our rule 'Do your best work.' Move to this other group for the rest of class today, and you can try working with Meg again tomorrow."

- **Realistic**—The consequence must be something that a student can accomplish and that you can follow through on. For example, if a student isn't paying attention during lunch and spills their lunch tray, cleaning up the resulting mess is a realistic consequence. Cleaning the whole cafeteria would be out of proportion to the mistake and would likely feel like a punishment rather than an opportunity for the student to learn from their mistake. It would also require an undue amount of time and effort from a teacher or other staff member to monitor.

By following these guidelines, you can give your best effort to making sure you react to misbehavior in a nonpunitive way. Still, there may be instances where students feel embarrassed about making a mistake or losing self-control, especially in the heightened self-consciousness of early adolescence. As a result, students may complain that you're picking on them or may resist a logical consequence. It's important to remember that we cannot control students' feelings but only do our best to be fair and help students get their behavior back on task as discreetly and with as much empathy as possible.

Types of Logical Consequences

There are three general types of logical consequences: loss of privilege; break it, fix it; and Space and Time. Although there are many ways in which they may be implemented, all logical consequences will usually fall into one of these categories. Which type of logical consequence you apply will depend not just on the situation, but on what you know about the student developmentally, academically, and socially.

- **Loss of privilege**—A privilege is an opportunity for students to learn to be responsible when acting autonomously, such as by using classroom equipment or supplies or by choosing their own partner to work with. When a student struggles to manage that responsibility—for example, by misusing supplies or continually joking around when they should be working—the privilege is removed for a brief period of time, generally a class period or a day. If a student is using a computer to watch sports highlights instead of researching their history project, they might lose computer privileges for the day and conduct research using print materials instead. It's important to convey that the privilege has not been removed forever, but that the student will have the opportunity to try again next time to engage in the appropriate behavior. It's also important to provide the student with an alternate way to continue with learning, such as by changing seats or using different materials.

- **Break it, fix it**—This type of consequence gives students the opportunity to fix or clean up something they've broken or spilled, whether on purpose or by accident. It reinforces the fact that we all make mistakes—not always out of anger or malice, but sometimes because we are being careless or forgetful—and that when we do, it's our responsibility to clean up after ourselves. For example, if a student is fooling around near the display table and breaks a classmate's diorama, the consequence of their actions could be to pick up any pieces that have fallen to the floor and offer to help the classmate fix the diorama.

- **Space and Time**—This logical consequence lets a student who is losing focus or having trouble controlling their words or actions go to a designated space in the classroom to calm down and refocus. Space and Time allows learning to continue while a student takes a break, and allows that student to rejoin the rest of the class in a way that is productive for everyone. For example, a student who has slammed their fist on the desk in frustration might go stand near the window, do some deep breathing exercises to calm down, and then return to their desk to continue the lesson when they are feeling back in control.

Introducing Logical Consequences to Students

It's important to introduce and discuss logical consequences before implementing them so that students understand their purpose and your good intentions. An open dialogue with students about their goals and how the rules help them achieve those goals can get the conversation started. Once you have reaffirmed the job of the rules in your learning community, ask students to consider what the consequences could be if any of these rules are broken. Their answers may include safety risks, hurt feelings, unfinished assignments, and interrupting others' ability to do their work.

Present the need for logical consequences by connecting them to students' answers about how the rules help them in their learning and what the risks are if rules aren't followed. Make it clear that mistakes are a natural part of the learning process, and that we all sometimes make mistakes, no matter how hard we try to follow the rules. Frame logical consequences as tools you will use to help students turn those mistakes into learning experiences. You may find it worthwhile to share some of your own mistakes and how you took responsibility for fixing them, such as by sweeping up the pieces of a glass you dropped on the floor so that nobody stepped on them and got hurt.

It can also be helpful to discuss how logical consequences guide other adults in their lives beyond school. For instance, you might discuss how if a professional chef spills olive oil all over the kitchen floor, they take the time to clean it up so no one slips. Or, if a team isn't performing at their best, their coach might call a time-out to help them regroup and refocus. There are many possible analogies you can use that can give students a vision of how logical consequences are there to help them succeed.

As part of the discussion, provide concrete, realistic examples of what these logical consequences might look like in your classroom. This will help students feel more at ease and more readily accept logical consequences when you use them. Consider the examples in the following chart, or make some up that more specifically relate to your rules and the scenarios students are likely to encounter in your classroom.

Using Logical Consequences

Misbehavior	Applicable rule	Logical consequence
A student accidentally knocks a stack of papers off of a neighboring table cluster.	Take care of school materials.	Break it, fix it: The student picks up the papers and asks if the group at the table cluster would like help getting them organized again.
While waiting to take a turn at bat, a student wildly swings a baseball bat around near where others are standing.	Be safe.	Loss of privilege: The student skips this turn and goes to the back of the line; they can try again their next time up.
In music class, a student who doesn't get the instrument they want tries to grab it away from the student who did get it.	Respect others.	Space and Time: The student takes a few minutes to calm down before choosing one of the available instruments.

Have students discuss these or other examples in small groups to consider how the actions relate to the rules and how the logical consequences connect to the actions. You might also give students other examples of misbehavior and have them name the associated rules and brainstorm possible logical consequences. Doing so can help them understand the thought process behind using logical consequences. However, be clear that in cases of actual misbehavior, the teacher is the one to determine the consequence, and that it is not negotiable.

IN THE CLASSROOM

Mr. Moral

After the class rules have been introduced, Mr. Moral holds a discussion about misbehavior. He uses an academic analogy to acknowledge that there will be times when students make mistakes. For example, when students first learned about graphing ordered pairs, they needed time to practice and would make errors along the way. As they continue to work on this skill, errors still occur sometimes, and that's okay. The same is true with rules.

Mr. Moral then explains that one of his jobs as their teacher is to help them follow the rules and to support them when they make mistakes, just as he would do with graphing ordered pairs. He frames mistakes as opportunities to learn how to get back on task. This leads to a discussion of ways he will respond to misbehavior throughout the year, which is a natural segue into introducing logical consequences.

After students have learned about the three types of logical consequences, they do a card activity to help them understand how those logical consequences might look when Mr. Moral uses them. In small groups, students receive cards featuring a variety of typical misbehaviors for sixth graders. Each group decides on a logical consequence that makes sense for the misbehavior on their card. Taking the time to introduce logical consequences in a developmentally appropriate way honors young adolescents' need to be involved and to understand the thinking behind how and why Mr. Moral will use logical consequences in the future.

Logical Consequences Scenarios

Scenario #1:
A student bumps into a classmate's desk and knocks some books onto the floor.
Applicable Rule(s)?
_____
Logical Consequence?
_____

Scenario #2:
Two students are whispering and giggling while working together on a social studies assignment.
Applicable Rule(s)?
_____
Logical Consequence?
_____

Scenario #3:
A student yells out ideas during a class discussion instead of raising their hand.
Applicable Rule(s)?
_____
Logical Consequence?
_____

Scenario #4:
A student is playing games on the computer instead of using it for research.
Applicable Rule(s)?
_____
Logical Consequence?
_____

Scenario #5:
Two students have a side conversation while a classmate is sharing.
Applicable Rule(s)?
_____
Logical Consequence?
_____

Scenario #6:
A student mishandles a microscope and damages it, causing their group to be unable to complete their science project.
Applicable Rule(s)?
_____
Logical Consequence?
_____

Scenario #7:
A student is distracting tablemates instead of working.
Applicable Rule(s)?
_____
Logical Consequence?
_____

Scenario #8:
A student is running in the hallway on the way to lunch.
Applicable Rule(s)?
_____
Logical Consequence?
_____

Scenario #9:
A student is working at another classmate's desk and makes marks on the desk with a pencil.
Applicable Rule(s)?
_____
Logical Consequence?
_____

Scenario #10:
Two students are talking while the principal is making morning announcements over the loudspeaker.
Applicable Rule(s)?
_____
Logical Consequence?
_____

Download a printable set of logical consequences scenario cards at
https://www.responsiveclassroom.org/printables/.

Teaching Space and Time

With loss of privilege and break it, fix it, the teacher decides what action the student should take in that moment. Space and Time is different in that it involves a specific set of procedures that will be consistent each time they're used. What Space and Time looks like in each classroom may be different: where to go, how to know when to go and when to come back, and what to do while there. That is why it is critical to use Interactive Modeling to show students what your expectations are.

Space and Time procedures to teach through Interactive Modeling include:

> Space and Time isn't for students who are "bad" but is a technique that they can use for their own benefit, both in and out of school.

- Going to a spot quickly and quietly

- Activities they might choose from in Space and Time, such as writing or drawing or using relaxation techniques, such as deep breathing

- Coming back from Space and Time quietly and rejoining the group without disrupting the learning

- Helping a classmate who is in Space and Time by leaving that person alone, going on with the classroom activity, and quietly welcoming the classmate back when they return

After you introduce Space and Time, give each student at least one opportunity to practice using it at a time when they are calm and focused. Let the class know you'll be doing this and will keep track of who has gone so that everyone gets a chance to practice. You may also want to let students know that you may sometimes take Space and Time yourself if you need a moment to refocus. This helps students see that Space and Time isn't for students who are "bad" but is a technique that they can use for their own benefit, both in and out of school.

When teaching expectations for Space and Time, here are a few additional things to consider:

- **Make the purpose clear.** Clarify that the intent of Space and Time is to give students a chance to calm down and regain self-control, not punish or embarrass them. To underscore this point, make it clear while modeling that you will direct students to take Space and Time as discreetly as possible. Also, emphasize that when a peer rejoins the group after taking Space and Time, that student will be welcome and learning will continue uninterrupted. This can help students see that the purpose truly is to help them regain self-control, and that once that objective is achieved, Space and Time is over. To further separate Space and Time from any punitive connotations, you might invite students to help you come up with a different name that reflects its positive purpose, such as "cool down" or "rest stop."

- **Give students options.** To further the concept that Space and Time isn't punishment, as well as to highlight students' responsibility, give students a few specific options for where to take Space and Time and what to do while they're there. Having choices gives students a certain amount of control and can help avoid power struggles. For example, you might give them an option of returning to their desk if they are not already sitting there, going to a Space and Time chair at the side of the room, or standing by the window. Do make sure that any areas for Space and Time are separate enough from the rest of the class that the student can get the distance they need, but close enough that they can still follow along with instruction and smoothly transition back when they're done. While in Space and Time, a student could have the option of taking deep breaths, using sensory materials, drawing, or doing some stretches.

IN THE CLASSROOM

Mr. Moral

A day or two after introducing the other two logical consequences, Mr. Moral introduces the concept of Space and Time by using a soccer game as an analogy: If a soccer player gets off-course or out of position during a game, the coach might substitute the player to give them a break. Mr. Moral explains to his class that Space and Time is similar—it is a tool in the classroom that can give them a break to recharge and refocus, just like a soccer player. Then, Mr. Moral uses Interactive Modeling to demonstrate how to go to Space and Time, discusses what other students should do when someone goes to Space and Time, and takes questions about Space and Time. He also posts a Space and Time anchor chart near the list of rules, together with anchor charts for the other logical consequences.

- **Use Space and Time promptly when you see a student start losing control.** To further protect students' dignity, it is incumbent upon teachers to pay attention to students' behavior and respond when they notice a student about to lose control, rather than waiting until they are already out of control. Small signals—such as muttering negative comments or repeatedly poking others—can be precursors to more disruptive behavior. Sending a student to Space and Time early maintains respect for that student by preserving the student's relationship with their classmates and making it easier for the student to regain self-control than it would be if things escalated. It also allows you to remain empathetic to that student—a much more difficult task once a student's behavior has risen to the level of verbal abuse or violence.

Mrs. Wylie

Mrs. Wylie teaches the routines for Space and Time early in the school year through Interactive Modeling. She starts by discussing situations in which Space and Time may be helpful, such as when a student is getting frustrated while working in a group. She then uses Interactive Modeling to teach students the procedures they'll need to follow, including using the sand timer located near the Space and Time area. Being able to keep track of the amount of time they spend in the Space and Time area lets students be independent about returning when time is up.

- **Keep instructions brief, clear, and calm.** Using a calm voice and neutral facial expression and body language when sending a student to Space and Time minimizes the possibility of class disruption. If necessary, take a moment before speaking so that you're able to maintain empathy and a respectful demeanor. You can also use a visual signal, such as pointing to a sign or spot in the classroom or handing the student a card. Model and practice such signals with students beforehand so they are clear on expectations.

- **Note that your instructions to take Space and Time are nonnegotiable.** A student might not always agree or realize that they need to take Space and Time, but make it clear that they should go anyway. Make yourself available after class or a later time to discuss why you sent the student to Space and Time and to hear what they have to say. Even if it turns out you misunderstood the situation, reinforce the student's positive actions in going to Space and Time.

■ IN THE CLASSROOM

Mrs. Wylie

Issues in Mrs. Wylie's class that can't be solved proactively or through teacher language usually involve students struggling to control their emotions. In these cases, Mrs. Wylie uses Space and Time to let students know that it's okay to be frustrated sometimes, and that there is a routine to help them deal with it and a place they can go to feel safe. The Space and Time area in Mrs. Wylie's class is called the relaxation

station. It is stocked with sensory materials such as worry stones and glitter wands. She also offers flexible seating, including a yoga ball, an Adirondack chair, and a wobble stool. Options give students more responsibility and independence, which helps to increase students' buy-in.

Mr. Abdus-Salaam

Space and Time in Mr. Abdus-Salaam's class is called the refill station. He uses a

- **Keep it brief and clarify who ends it.** The duration of Space and Time may fluctuate based on students' needs, but it is generally meant to be brief. The goal is for students to calm down and refocus, then rejoin the class when they are ready. Students who come back too early can immediately become a disruption to learning, while other students might take advantage of the time away by lingering longer than necessary. When modeling Space and Time, make it clear to students whether you will be deciding when it's over or if they will, or if you will make a timer available to allow them to go for a set amount of time. It can be effective to start off making those decisions yourself until students are ready for the responsibility. If you are in charge of letting a student know when they can return, a simple signal, such as a nod or hand signal, protects the student's self-esteem by not drawing attention to their return while also allowing the class to continue their work uninterrupted. Later, help students learn to interpret their own physical and emotional signals so that they understand when they're ready to come back.

- **Use Space and Time democratically.** It's important for students to see that everyone occasionally needs the opportunity to step away so that they can calm down and refocus, not just the same handful of students. It's also important for them to see that Space and Time is used for subtle behaviors—such as when a student is just beginning to act out, lose focus, or get stressed out—not just the more noticeable misbehaviors. This shows students that Space and Time is a necessary strategy for all students.

- **Be a good role model for regaining self-control.** Show students that taking a moment to calm down is a useful skill they can use both now and as adults. Take Space and Time yourself if you need it, and let students know in advance that you may do so. This further underscores the fact that this logical consequence is designed to help them, not punish them.

basketball analogy to help students understand how it supports their learning. Just as a basketball team uses time-outs to catch their breath, the refill station gives students a chance to regroup. The station is in a corner of the room so students have some privacy. They are given the responsibility of deciding when to return to learning. While there is no time limit, students generally remain there for two to three minutes. If a student takes a lot longer or ends up

there multiple times in a class period, Mr. Abdus-Salaam checks in with the student privately to see what's going on and what might help them.

Mr. Moral
Mr. Moral offers students the opportunity to rename Space and Time. One class renamed it take a break, and another chose the name chill chair, though most classes just stick with Space and Time.

Additional Tips

Here are some other considerations to keep in mind when using logical consequences.

The Teacher Chooses the Consequence

During your introductory discussion of logical consequences, having students come up with appropriate consequences for various hypothetical situations can help them understand the purpose of this way of handling misbehavior and get a sense of what to expect. However, in actual rule-breaking situations, you are in charge of deciding on the consequence. Choosing an appropriate consequence requires the judgment and wisdom that we as teachers bring to the classroom. It is also not a suitable task for students who are misbehaving, as they are not in control in the moment and therefore are not in the right state to think rationally about the right consequence.

> Like any other skill, assigning logical consequences requires practice in order to feel natural.

It may take you some time before you feel comfortable making these decisions. Like any other skill, assigning logical consequences requires practice in order to feel natural. Be patient with yourself as you hone your instincts about what is appropriate for each situation.

One Size Does Not Fit All

Every student is unique. Consider what you know socially, emotionally, and academically about the students you teach. Also consider the developmental patterns of young adolescents and the fact that their growth is uneven—on a day-to-day basis their needs and maturity levels can fluctuate. In addition, each situation is unique. Thus, it's important to consider the whole picture when assigning logical consequences rather than using a predetermined standard response.

Researchers have found that when our psychological needs aren't met, we often behave in negative ways. These needs include feeling a sense of belonging and significance (Dreikurs, Grunwald, and Pepper 1982). Ask yourself whether a student might be feeling left out or unrecognized, and how you might support their good behavior by helping them feel a stronger sense of connection with the classroom community. Students also need to feel a sense of autonomy and competence (Deci 1995), so it's important to consider whether they have adequate opportunities to take responsibility for their own learning and to demonstrate their abilities.

Here are a few other questions to ask yourself that might help you determine the right approach for responding to a particular student's misbehavior:

- Did I set expectations clearly? Are those expectations too high or too low?

- Is this behavior part of a pattern or is it an isolated incident?

- Is this student testing the limits or looking for ways to assert their own power?

- What has worked for this student in the past? What hasn't been helpful?

The goal is not to uniformly apply logical consequences, but to take into account what motivates a student and what they understand about the rules in order to choose a consequence that will best support their continued behavioral growth. Being consistent builds trust with students, but consistency comes from always intervening firmly but calmly when any student misbehaves, not from employing the same consequence regardless of context.

Predetermined Consequences May Be Appropriate Sometimes

As noted above, each student and situation is unique. However, there may be times when a particular consequence is needed, especially when it comes to protecting students' safety. For example, you might decide that any student who misuses sharp dissection tools during a science lab immediately loses that privilege for the rest of the lab. It's up to each teacher to decide what situations require these kinds of standardized consequences.

If the Connection Isn't Obvious, the Consequence Is Probably Not Logical

When determining a logical consequence to use in a given situation, take a few moments to consider: What do you know about this student? What appears to be the root of the problem? What can you do to help this student understand and fix the misbehavior? If a logical consequence doesn't become apparent after answering these questions, it might not be the best strategy for addressing this particular situation. In some situations, a logical consequence may not be needed at all. For example, if a student forgets the permission slip they need to watch a movie in your classroom, the natural consequence of missing the movie is enough of a lesson. No further response is required.

Keep the Time Between Misbehavior and Consequence Minimal

It can be helpful to take a moment to pause and consider which logical consequence to use and ensure that it's respectful, related, and realistic. However, waiting too long can allow misbehavior to escalate and can stand in the way of students seeing how the logical consequence is connected to the behavior. Apply consequences as quickly as you can thoughtfully and calmly do so.

Two Steps Are Sometimes Needed

There may be situations in which more than one logical consequence is required, often because either the student needs to calm down or we do. Stopping the misbehavior and sending the student (or ourselves) to Space and Time, if appropriate, is the first step. After everyone is calmer, if we feel that a loss of privilege is needed or something has been broken that needs to be fixed, we can assign a second consequence.

Break it, fix it works best in the moment when a student has honestly made a mistake, not when they are upset, losing control, or purposefully acting out against the rules. That student either needs Space and Time in order to calm down and regain control, or loss of privilege until they are ready to reengage with the activity or materials. In either case, only once the student has calmed down will they have the necessary mindset to take responsibility for fixing damage they have caused.

"Fixing it" can also be done figuratively, such as to mend hurt feelings after being unkind to someone. However, this may also require waiting until the heat of the moment has passed. Young adolescents value the opinion of their peers above almost anything else and have a lot of influence over one another, so when one student hurts another's feelings, emotions are generally running high for all parties involved. Time to regain composure is critical in order for the students involved to respond appropriately to each other. After everyone has cooled down, "fixing it" might entail students working productively together or using kind words toward each other. It might also involve one student apologizing to another, though it's important never to force students to apologize. Authentic apologies require reflection and should only be offered voluntarily in order to ensure that they are genuine.

Keep Explanations Brief

Use as few words as possible when using a logical consequence, and let the consequence speak for itself. Having a more prolonged discussion may give students the mistaken idea that the consequence is negotiable. Also, trying in the moment to explain what a student did wrong can escalate the situation, especially if emotions are running high. Reserve such explanations for later, once everyone is calm and ready to have a productive conversation.

Collaborate With Colleagues

Working with your teaching team or other educators in your school can provide insights about students and opportunities for brainstorming solutions to tricky behavior problems. Such conversations can reveal clues as to why students behave the way they do and how to help them. Do they act differently in different environments, or is the misbehavior consistent in all classes? Are there particular techniques that have proven helpful in the past? Talking to teachers from other teams can also be beneficial, as they may have objective distance that allows them to see the situation more clearly. Effective solutions often arise from the collective wisdom of experienced and passionate teachers.

Have a Reentry Check-In if a Student Leaves the Room

In some cases, a student needs to leave the room in order to effectively cool down, perhaps to take a walk to the water fountain or go see the guidance counselor. In these cases, take a moment to check in with them when they return so that you can make sure they're ready to come back and reassure them that your rapport is intact. Make sure they know what to do now, and allow them to ask questions or communicate their side of things to you if they need to before returning to the classroom activity.

Encourage Students to Take Responsibility for Themselves

As students move through early adolescence, they take on more responsibilities in school and in their lives in general. Part of that increased level of responsibility means taking charge of their own behavior. As time goes on, look for and encourage students to begin correcting their own mistakes when possible. Just as we hope a student will begin to understand how to solve a math problem or use an app correctly after we explain it a few times, students will hopefully begin to understand how they can take responsibility for their actions after you've been using logical consequences for a while. Discreetly reinforce their efforts when you see someone clean up a mess they've made, move to a seat away from a chatty friend who's distracting them, or take a moment to calm themselves down when they become frustrated.

Keep Practicing

Just as students need to practice, make mistakes, and learn from those mistakes in both their academics and their behavior, we as teachers need to do the same to improve how we respond to misbehavior. Handling misbehavior can be one of the biggest challenges of teaching, so it's to be expected that doing it well will require practice. Show yourself the same empathy you show your students, and know that you will have many opportunities for improvement over time.

■ IN THE CLASSROOM

Mrs. Wylie

A maxim that Mrs. Wylie lives by is that every moment is a new moment and every student gets a new opportunity to be who they want to be. She knows that adolescents are trying to figure out the world as their brains grow and develop in incredible ways. They might be completely different in 20 minutes! Pigeonholing them in any way only stunts their growth.

Addressing Bias to Ensure That Discipline Is Fair

One other critical goal of responding to misbehavior is to make sure your responses are fair for all students. One middle school teacher remembers a time when many of the boys in her eighth grade class would act up every day, and she would either ignore their misbehavior or simply give them a warning. One day, one of the girls was acting up, and the teacher gave her lunch detention. But the girl called out the disparity—she was only doing what the boys always did, so why did she get a harsher punishment? Only then did this teacher realize she had been treating her students differently based on their gender, and she knew she needed to be more careful to ensure fair treatment for everyone.

We may all have times when we don't treat students fairly, whether or not we realize it. Even though we may not mean any harm, these discrepancies can lead to dramatic effects on students' behavior, academic performance, and sense of self-worth. Thus, it is critical that we examine our own behavior and change where needed to ensure an equitable experience for all the students we teach.

Unconscious Bias

While we may have the best of intentions to treat all students fairly, we are all susceptible to basing our actions on stereotypes that we aren't aware of having. This phenomenon, known as unconscious bias (Dee and Gershenson 2017), affects everyone. It means that the brain's natural ability for pattern recognition sometimes picks up on negative patterns in the messages we grew up with, internalized, and continue to absorb through popular culture and the world around us. And if we react to students' behavior based on those negative patterns, we may not treat all students fairly. That's why it's so important to examine the way we react to students and identify any disparities in our reactions based on race, gender, disability, or other characteristics.

The wide variety of factors that influence our unconscious beliefs may not be within our control, but the way our beliefs shape our interactions with students is something we can change. Indeed, it is our responsibility to examine these beliefs and minimize any negative effects they have on our discipline practices or other actions in the classroom (Kirwan Institute 2015). One of the most effective ways to keep from acting based on stereotypical beliefs is to get to know students as individuals rather than as typical members of a particular group. Through formal activities or casual discussions, talk to students about their lives, interests, families, and cultures. The goal-setting process (see pages 47–51) offers an excellent opportunity to learn about what matters most to students as individuals.

Not only must we know the students in our classes but we must also know ourselves. Looking deeper into our own behaviors and beliefs is essential to helping us recognize our biases and keeping them from negatively influencing our students and the learning that goes on in our classrooms. The process below outlines steps we can take to know ourselves better and more consciously shape our behavior as teachers.

1 **Recognize and accept that we all have unconscious biases.** As open-minded as we may strive to be, we all experience this phenomenon and all have work to do in being more mindful about our behavior. Rather than getting defensive about this fact, which can stop this process in its tracks, it's important to accept that while it can be unsettling and uncomfortable to think about one's biases, it is important and necessary work.

2 **Question yourself and your behaviors.** Each day, take a few minutes to reflect on your interactions with students. Think about the following questions:

■ Are my thoughts, expectations, behaviors, and interactions based on objective observation, data, and realistic assessments of all students' strengths and challenges?

■ What evidence do I have to support how I am behaving in my classroom and treating individual students?

■ When I greet students at the door, do I welcome all students warmly? Does my greeting let all students know that I care about them and am glad to see them today?

■ Do I interact with all students using a neutral, calm stance and tone? Or do I shift my stance with certain students (crossing arms across chest, putting hands on hips, moving closer or farther away, etc.)?

■ Do I value every student's comments the same by showing interest and making eye contact with them?

■ Do I call on all students, or only an eager few?

■ What message does my verbal language convey? Do I offer reinforcement to all students? Do I remind and redirect all students?

3 **As you become aware, catch yourself behaving in ways that reflect an unconscious bias.** If you notice yourself responding unfairly to a student or if they react to you in a way that suggests you have, make a point to correct yourself. Pay attention to how you feel as you see students behaving in certain ways. Do you find yourself becoming more quickly frustrated or impatient with one student over another, even though both are behaving in the same way? When you do experience these feelings, take a moment to calm down before reacting so that you can be sure you're about to think rationally. Take note of the patterns you witness in yourself, and set achievable goals for improvement. To start with, identify a single behavior that you believe comes from an unconscious bias, and set a goal of reducing it by a certain amount by a particular deadline. For example, if you realize you've been calling on boys to read their work aloud more frequently than girls, set up a system for ensuring that you give everyone a chance, such as making a list of everyone in the class and checking off each name as they are called on, making sure that every name is checked before calling on someone to read a second time.

4 **Commit to ongoing work on this issue.** It isn't easy to examine one's own biases, and there isn't a quick fix for reducing the effects of bias in our classrooms. We must make an ongoing commitment to examine our own beliefs honestly and keep setting higher goals for our own behavior. Continue to watch for any biased behavior that slips into your practice in the classroom, and keep learning about the students you teach. In addition, commit to

> We must make an ongoing commitment to examine our own beliefs honestly and keep setting higher goals for our own behavior.

learning about people who are different than you in terms of culture, gender, ability, and other ways so that you can continue to broaden your perspective and break down stereotypical beliefs. Work with other educators to examine how unconscious bias affects the students in your school and to minimize its impact. Pairing up with a member of your teaching team or another colleague to observe each other's body language, words, and interactions with students can be illuminating and lead to real change.

Stereotype Threat

One of the negative effects unconscious bias can have if left unchecked is stereotype threat: the phenomenon in which a student forms a self-image based on others' negative perceptions and assumptions, and subsequently acts in accordance with those assumptions (Reducing Stereotype Threat, n.d.). For example, an unconscious bias that students with physical disabilities are less capable of doing rigorous academic work may lead a teacher to call on those students less frequently or give them simpler tasks to do. As a result, the students may grow to see themselves as less capable and act in accordance with that self-image—for example, by putting forth less effort on their assignments.

Not only do we need to change our own behaviors and examine our own beliefs but we also must help students see themselves in a positive light. One way to do this is through teacher language. Use reinforcing language (pages 23–24) to help students recognize and build on their accomplishments and abilities, and envisioning language (page 22) to allow them to visualize and achieve positive outcomes, both in and out of school.

Another important strategy is assessing the materials you use with your classes. Consider the posters and other visuals on your walls, the characters and stories in the books you assign, and the authors and experts whose materials you use during lessons. Do all students get to see themselves reflected in these images and stories?

Are the people who look like them and come from similar backgrounds portrayed in positive ways as competent individuals, or in stereotypical ways? These materials speak as loudly as your own words and actions in terms of conveying your beliefs about students.

There are also activities you can do with your classes to bolster students' sense of self and reduce stereotype threat. These activities offer opportunities to practice self-affirmation, which can achieve several goals associated with decreasing stereotype threat (Cascio et al. 2015). The following chart lists these goals with a sample activity for each.

Reducing Stereotype Threat

Goal	Activity
Help students recognize and affirm their own positive attributes.	**I Am**—Have students name three to five positive adjectives to describe themselves, such as "friendly," "thoughtful," "determined," and "brave." Then, have students draw a picture or write a story that shows them acting out these characteristics.
Provide examples of positive role models across diverse demographic groups.	**I Can**—Have students identify someone they admire from a demographic group they belong to. This could be a community leader, an educator, or someone else who has achieved success in their field. Then, ask students to identify three positive characteristics about that person. Students can draw or write about how they, too, might become a role model in the future.
Build resilience in the face of adversity.	**I Will**—Share ways that prominent role models have overcome adversity on the road to success, and give examples from your own life, too. With these stories fresh in students' minds, use open-ended questions to help students generate ideas about how to face the challenges in their lives and see themselves as capable of overcoming those challenges.
Foster a growth mindset.	**I Learn**—Help students see that intelligence and abilities are not fixed but can be developed and strengthened with time and practice. Share examples of successful individuals in a variety of careers, and discuss the types of skills those people needed to learn and practice in order to achieve success. Also, ask students about their own skills, and have them reflect on the process of building those skills through practice and learning from mistakes.

Along with this chapter's other guidelines for maintaining empathy, curiosity, and a belief in students' good intentions, the techniques in this section can help you ensure that your discipline practices are fair and effective for all students. It will take time to do this work, so be patient yet persistent as you forge ahead. Seek support from colleagues, keep an open mind, and remember how crucial this work can be in helping the students you teach succeed now and in their future lives.

Responding to Misbehavior

1 Students misbehave for many reasons related to their own needs and impulses, and they need practice to learn how to meet behavior expectations.

2 When responding to misbehavior, the primary goals are to stop the behavior so that learning can continue, help students understand the consequences of their actions and develop self-regulation, and preserve the dignity of the student and the group.

3 The three types of logical consequences (loss of privilege; break it, fix it; and Space and Time) offer respectful, related, and realistic ways to help students practice self-control, learn from their mistakes, and fix any damage their actions may have caused.

4 Examining one's own biases and taking steps to ensure fairness toward all students are essential practices as we teach discipline.

References

Cascio, Christopher N., Matthew Brook O'Donnell, Francis J. Tinney, Matthew D. Lieberman, Shelley E. Taylor, Victor J. Strecher, and Emily B. Falk. 2016. "Self-Affirmation Activates Brain Systems Associated With Self-Related Processing and Reward and Is Reinforced by Future Orientation." *Social Cognitive and Affective Neuroscience* 11, no. 4 (April): 621–629. https://doi.org/10.1093/scan/nsv136.

Deci, Edward L. (with Richard Flaste). 1995. *Why We Do What We Do.* New York: Penguin.

Dreikurs, Rudolf, Bernice Bronia Grunwald, and Floy C. Pepper. 1982. *Maintaining Sanity in the Classroom: Classroom Management Techniques.* 2nd ed. New York: Harper and Row.

Dee, Thomas and Seth Gershenson. 2017. "Unconscious Bias in the Classroom: Evidence and Opportunities." Google's Computer Science Education Research.

Kirwan Institute. n.d. "Strategies for Addressing Implicit Bias in Early Childhood Education." Accessed July 9, 2018. http://kirwaninstitute.osu.edu/wp-content/uploads/2015/06/implicitbias-strategies.pdf.

Reducing Stereotype Threat. n.d. "What Is Stereotype Threat?" Accessed July 9, 2018. http://www.reducingstereotypethreat.org/what-is-stereotype-threat-2/.

Problem:

Solution:

88

Solving Ongoing Problem Behavior

Solving Ongoing Problem Behavior

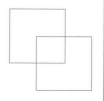

Logical consequences are an effective way to respond to individual incidents of misbehavior in a way that helps students build self-regulation skills. However, when a student repeatedly exhibits the same misbehavior, such as making sarcastic comments or playing with materials instead of using them appropriately, logical consequences may not be the right technique for addressing the issue. In these cases, a one-time common misbehavior has turned into ongoing problem behavior that gets in the way of academics, relationships, or both, and it needs to be handled in a different way.

The strategies outlined in this chapter rely on teacher-student collaboration to handle problem behaviors. Using these methods, students and teachers work together to identify the root causes of a particular problem behavior and generate solutions that will work for the students involved. To be successful with these methods, it is essential to maintain empathy, as we can only truly collaborate with students when we are being empathetic. It can be tempting to take problem behavior personally, but empathy allows us to see the misbehaving student just as we might see them struggling in any academic area—as a student who needs extra time and attention in order to succeed.

IN THE CLASSROOM

Mrs. Wylie

Empathy is central to how Mrs. Wylie responds to behavior issues. Knowing that ongoing misbehavior often results from a deeper issue, she looks for the root of the problem. She communicates with parents to see if there is anything going on outside of school she should know about, and visits other classrooms to observe the student and see what is happening in that setting that isn't happening in her classroom. She also asks the student directly, "What can I do to help?" This puts her and the student on the same level, effectively communicating to the student that "we are in this together." Nine times out of ten, in Mrs. Wylie's experience, students respond when they know the teacher cares.

Checking the Foundations of Good Behavior

If you're seeing persistent misbehavior in one or more students in a class, take some time before moving beyond logical consequences to gather information about what may be happening. For example, if you notice multiple students struggling with the same misbehavior, it might be time for a refresher discussion about the rules and why they are important. Using Interactive Modeling to remind students of the established expectations can also help refocus students who have gotten away from performing classroom routines and procedures in the way they should. It's common to find that these refreshers are needed in the middle of the school year or semester and after students come back from a school break or vacation.

Assessing yourself can be just as informative as assessing student behavior. Have you been using teacher language in a consistent and effective way to help students envision positive outcomes, reinforce their good behavior, remind them of expectations, and redirect them when they get off task? Also, take a look at how you have been enforcing the rules. Have you been diligent in responding at the first sign of misbehavior? Has your use of logical consequences been swift, consistent, and fair? Sometimes all that is needed to address a behavior problem is an adjustment in our own practices.

In addition, it's a good idea to consider students' basic needs. For instance:

- **Think about their physical needs.** If a student comes to school hungry, they are more likely to act out or have trouble focusing. Are you able to keep snacks on hand for students who need them? Or, if you notice that students seem antsy or have low energy at the same time every day, it could be a sign that they need more movement or social interaction. Adding a quick brain break to that part of the day could help them focus their energy.

- **Consider students' needs for belonging and significance.** Are you recognizing students for their accomplishments? Is the climate of your classroom community one that encourages acceptance and affiliation among students?

- **Look at students' social-emotional skills.** Do they need additional instruction or practice to help them strengthen the competencies of cooperation, assertiveness, responsibility, empathy, or self-control? One way to support these skills is by using books or human interest stories and asking students questions about those situations. How might they respond if they were in the situation the character is in? Do they think the person in the story showed responsibility or empathy? Why or why not? How could they have done things better? Through stories that aren't directly about the students in the room, you can allow for discussion about these skills in ways that won't make students self-conscious. You might even have them come up with their own stories or scenarios in which particular social-emotional skills are demonstrated.

- **Take students' developmental levels into account** and how their development may have progressed since you first started working with them. In some phases, students need more activity or social engagement than in others.

- **Think about how well your lesson plans are working.** Are they designed to engage and challenge students? Look for patterns in terms of when during lessons misbehavior typically occurs to help you diagnose its source.

 To learn more about using brain breaks, see *Refocus and Recharge! 50 Brain Breaks for Middle Schoolers* (Center for Responsive Schools, 2016).

Once you've checked that students' basic needs are being met and that they are clear on class routines, procedures, and expectations—and that you're calmly but firmly enforcing those expectations—it might be time to move on to a different strategy to address persistent misbehavior. Problem-solving conferences are a useful way to find solutions with individual students who are exhibiting a problem behavior, while structured class meetings can help a whole group that is having difficulty with a particular issue.

Whichever strategies you use, strategizing and collaborating with your teaching team or other school staff, such as counselors, the special education team, and social workers, can help everyone better support a struggling student. Your colleagues may know the students you teach and be able to provide insights and ideas for working with them. Other educators can also practice the techniques in this chapter with you so that you feel confident in using them in your classroom.

■ IN THE CLASSROOM

Mr. Abdus-Salaam

The grade-level teachers in Mr. Abdus-Salaam's school are constantly collaborating. Along with regularly having lunch together, they schedule Monday morning conversations where they can discuss what's working and not working with their approach, and how to improve it.

Mr. Moral

Mr. Moral's grade level team and the school's lunch staff all use the same common quiet signal—an auditory chime and a raised hand. This collaboration between adults promotes consistency and clear expectations for students throughout school, making it easier for them to understand and meet expectations.

Problem-Solving Conferences

Every student is unique, and the solution to a single type of problem behavior may vary greatly from student to student. For example, one student who often acts silly and makes jokes when others are speaking might need a signal from the teacher to help them focus, while another student might benefit from a different seating arrangement so they aren't near friends who set them off, or alternate opportunities to express their sense of humor. Finding the right solution for a given student is key, and that's where problem-solving conferences come in.

A problem-solving conference is a one-on-one structured meeting where a student and teacher work together to determine the cause of a problem behavior and brainstorm ways to address it. Giving the student a say in solving the problem helps them gradually take on more responsibility for monitoring and correcting their own behavior, and helps them learn strategies for preventing or solving issues in the future. This collaborative process can also give you important insights into the student's needs that you might not be able to come up with on your own. The conference should take about 10 to 15 minutes and may be scheduled before or after school, as a private lunch, or at another time that's convenient for both you and the student.

Before you meet with a student, think about some possible causes of the behavior and what might help resolve it. For example, a student who regularly wanders around the room during collaborative work might not be engaged due to the work being too easy or too challenging, or they may physically need more activity in their day. Depending on the cause, potential solutions might include working with them individually to learn strategies for staying focused, or giving them opportunities to be more physically active by using a standing desk or stretching at their desk while they collaborate. You might also talk to your teaching teammates or other colleagues who know the student to get their input. However, it is important to remain open to what the student has to say. They may express a different root cause than what you imagined—for example, they may be walking around to calm down due to stressful events at home that are on their mind—and therefore need a very different type of solution. Keeping teacher talk to a minimum will leave space for the student to express themselves openly and honestly.

Follow these steps to lead an effective problem-solving conference:

1 **Establish the purpose of the conference.** The first step is to let the student know why you've called the conference, and that you want to work with the student to help them succeed. For example, you might say, "I want to talk with you about some things I've noticed during writing workshop." Make sure to keep the discussion focused on the primary issue. If the student brings up issues they're experiencing other than the one on which the conference is focused, let them know that you can talk about those at a different time.

2 **Reaffirm teacher-student rapport.** To reinforce that you are both on the same side, reaffirm the positive relationship you already have with the student by noting their efforts and recent successes in your class: "You had some truly interesting insights today about the book we're reading." When students see that we believe in them, are paying attention to them, and have faith in their abilities to succeed in school, they are more likely to invest in the collaborative process of finding a solution to a problem. (If it feels more natural, you can do this step first.)

3 **Name the problematic behavior.** When bringing up the problem behavior, use a calm tone and be specific, brief, and matter-of-fact. Then, ask the student what they've noticed. "We've talked about it a few times in the moment, but I've heard you using some unkind language with your writing workshop group. What have you noticed?" They may be aware of their behavior and be able to provide some insight into why it's happening. Or, it may be that this is the first time it has come to their attention. Either way, it is essential that you both agree the issue is occurring. If the student doesn't see the behavior as a problem, a problem-solving conference isn't the right solution. The student first needs more help understanding classroom rules and expectations. Assuming the student does acknowledge the problem,

■ IN THE CLASSROOM

Mr. Moral
In addition to holding one-on-one problem-solving conferences with students, Mr. Moral offers them the option to bring in a second teacher with whom they feel comfortable. Even if the problem behavior is happening exclusively in Mr. Moral's classroom, having another teacher from the team there helps some students feel more supported and more willing to collaborate. The steps of the problem-solving conference are the same, but with an additional teacher there to listen and help brainstorm solutions.

ask them what they think might be causing it. Clearly explain why you'd like to help and how you see addressing this problem improving the student's life at school: "I know your goal this semester is to make some new friends, and I want to help you find success in doing that. Making sure you're speaking respectfully is going to support you in achieving that goal."

4 **Invite the student to collaborate with you.** Once you have both shared your perspectives on what's happening and agreed that a problem exists, invite the student to collaborate with you on possible solutions. "Would you like some help figuring out how to work on this?" If the student does not want to collaborate, you may need to work on strengthening your relationship with them before using a problem-solving conference with them. Being an empathetic listener in this situation and truly hearing what the student has to say will help them feel safe discussing the problem and working with you to find a solution.

5 **Set a goal and generate strategies.** The teacher's role in this step is to act as a facilitator to help the student come up with possible strategies to try. Start by setting a goal, and then help the student brainstorm ideas for how to achieve it: "So, if your goal is to use more respectful language in writing workshop, what are some things you could try to help you get there?" Let the student choose which option they'd like to try, discuss how they will know whether it's working, and set a date and time to follow up on their progress. When you reconvene, ask how they feel they've been doing, reinforce the progress you've seen, and discuss whether the current strategy is working or they would like to try a new one.

Class Meetings

When a problem behavior is more widespread, a class meeting may be in order to talk about the problem and come up with solutions as a group. This practice lets everyone in the room have a voice in discussing the problem, how it affects them, and how to fix it. Class meetings are appropriate when many members of the group aren't behaving according to the rules; if only one or a few students are exhibiting the problem behavior, it's better to approach only the individuals involved. Also, class meetings are only useful in situations where you're open to student ideas. If you have one specific way you want the problem solved, use Interactive Modeling to teach or remind students about your expectations.

In some cases, bringing students together in a circle can be a powerful way to discuss important topics, as the circle offers everyone in the group the opportunity to be seen and heard. Just as people from many different cultures throughout history have come together in a circle to feel connected with one another, you can take advantage of this simple yet powerful structure to increase connection among everyone in the room. By enabling everyone to make eye contact with one another, the circle helps everyone focus on the discussion at hand and feel included. And having everyone sit or stand together without hierarchy creates a space that is ideal for discussing conflicts or other difficult situations. However, there may be cases where it is more productive to allow students to remain at their desks or table clusters for a class meeting if being able to see and make eye contact with everyone will make students feel too vulnerable to participate productively. Use your judgment about the class and the situation at hand to help you determine the best structure for your class meeting.

Allow about five to eight minutes for the meeting, and try to schedule it either at the beginning of the class period or just before a particular lesson where the problem has been occurring. This will allow students to practice the solution they come up with during class.

1 **State the reason for the meeting.** Start on a positive note, and then let students know what you've been seeing that has prompted you to call the meeting: "Everyone has been very enthusiastic lately, and you have a lot of great ideas to share! I have noticed that a lot of the time, people are calling out answers without raising their hand and sometimes speaking over each other."

This practice lets everyone in the room have a voice in discussing the problem, how it affects them, and how to fix it.

2 **Connect the problem to the rules.** State how the problem behavior doesn't follow the class rules: "It's important that everyone gets a chance to be heard in this class. That's one way you can follow our rule to 'Respect other people.'"

3 **Invite students' input with open-ended questions.** Ask for volunteers to share what they've noticed or how this issue has affected them. If the topic is more sensitive or you feel your class would be more open if their answers were anonymous, you can have students write down their answers on slips of paper, and then you can read out a few: "Sometimes I feel like I never get to talk." "It gets really loud in here, and it's hard to think." "If I don't say my idea right away, I forget it."

4 **Ask for potential solutions to the problem.** Elicit possible solutions from the class: "What are some ideas you have to help people hold their thought until they're called on?" Again, you can do this step by asking volunteers to share ideas aloud or by having students write ideas on slips of paper that you then read to the class: "We could write the idea on a sticky note and share it later." "People could try to only talk twice during each class and then just listen."

5 **Choose a solution to try.** Pick one idea to start with. "What if we tried writing the idea on a sticky note? Let's take a vote—everyone put your thumb up if you want to try it, thumb to the side if you can live with it, or thumb down if you can't live with it." If there are any "can't live with it" votes, discuss how you might modify the idea or use a different idea.

Watch for students to demonstrate the solution throughout the following class period. You can then follow up at the end of class with reinforcement and feedback: "People were writing down all their great ideas on sticky notes and sharing them when I asked for responses. That allowed for many voices to be heard today." You can also use envisioning language to tell students how you see this solution helping them in the long term: "Being able to hold your thoughts until it's appropriate to share them is an important way to practice self-control. That's going to help you in all of your classes and your relationships."

In the coming days and weeks, keep following up and reinforcing progress. If the chosen solution isn't getting the results you'd hoped for, try a new one. You can either choose from one of the previously suggested possibilities or work with the class to generate new ideas.

If the problem behavior is occurring in different classes throughout the team and is affecting the whole team, it's a good idea to plan a whole-team meeting as opposed to a single-class meeting, perhaps at the beginning of the day. Some problems originate outside the classroom entirely: on the bus, in the cafeteria, or elsewhere in the neighborhood. Work together with the other teachers on your team to plan the timing, topic, and structure of these meetings. You might also bring in any elective or exploratory teachers or guidance staff who have been involved with managing the problem behavior, or you might communicate the outcomes of the meeting to them privately afterward.

Talking to Parents About Problem Behavior

Parents can be among your greatest allies when helping students with problem behavior. Regular communication gives parents important information about how their children are doing in school, and it can also provide you with insights to help you better understand and work with those students.

You may find it helpful to collaborate with your teaching team about how best to reach out to parents. If a student is demonstrating a particular problem behavior in multiple classes, consider having a joint conference with the parents or selecting one teacher to call the parents on behalf of the whole team. It's also useful to build rapport with parents as a team to offer consistent messages and give parents confidence that the whole team is working together to help their child.

Consider the tips below to help you have productive conversations with parents about their children's behavior:

- **Build the relationship before problem behavior starts.** Discussing behavior challenges with parents works best when you've already established a strong foundation of communication and mutual respect with them. The earlier this is done in the school year, the stronger that foundation will be. Reaching out in the weeks leading up to the start of school can lay the groundwork for this relationship. Consider getting in touch by phone or email or hosting regular conferences or open houses to get to know parents better, especially in the early days and weeks of the school year. This outreach indicates to parents that you care about their child's success, and it generates a sense of warmth and trust. As the year goes on, get in touch regularly with positive updates. This will help them understand that you're on their child's side, and will lessen any apprehension they may have about getting a call from their child's teacher.

- **Reach out early when you notice a pattern of problem behavior.** If a small problem escalates into a bigger one or goes on for a long time, parents may feel frustrated or angry that they didn't know about it sooner. Contact them as soon as a pattern becomes apparent, and let them know what you've noticed and how you're working to help their child. There may be times when parents can even reinforce your strategies at home, such as by encouraging their child to practice techniques that you've taught them for reducing test anxiety.

■ **Have a clear purpose in mind.** When you reach out to parents, make sure you know what it is you want out of the interaction. Are you simply informing them of what's going on with their child? Have you noticed a sudden change in a student's behavior and you're wondering if something is happening outside of school? Are you looking for parents to help you in some way? Make it clear that your intention isn't to blame parents or pass off a problem for them to solve on their own.

■ **Let parents know you like their child and genuinely want to help them.** Start by mentioning some of the positive things you've observed the student doing in your classroom. This helps parents see that you are committed to their child's growth.

■ **Keep the conversation focused on facts.** When you do explain the problematic behavior, avoid labels. Instead, focus on a specific and succinct summary of the behavior in question. "Lea sometimes struggles to stay focused on her work" is more productive than "Lea is always daydreaming and never pays attention." The former statement puts the emphasis on the behavior rather than judging or criticizing the student or their personality. It may help to provide evidence of the incident in question, if you have it, such as an unkind note written from the student to a peer. This steers the conversation away from your attempting to convince a parent of what happened, so instead, it can focus on solutions. Also, do your best to maintain a calm state of mind during the discussion. A frustrated or annoyed tone can understandably cause a parent to feel protective of their child, which can put them in a defensive mood rather than a collaborative one.

■ **Discuss how the behavior might harm the student.** Knowing specifically how a problem behavior may negatively impact their child—rather than thinking it simply annoys the teacher—can help parents feel more invested in wanting to fix the problem. For example, you might say, "I'm afraid that Cecilia's excluding others at lunch may keep her from making some new friends, and it may be alienating some of her current friends, as well."

■ **IN THE CLASSROOM**

Mrs. Wylie

To keep in touch with parents and family, Mrs. Wylie uses an app that parents can sign up for called Remind: School Communication. Parents who use this app know where to reach her, and she can use it to send out group messages about upcoming school activities or notes to individual parents. These lines of communication make it easier and more convenient for Mrs. Wylie to extend the sense of community beyond the classroom.

Solving Ongoing Problem Behavior

1 Before moving to other strategies for managing problem behavior, make sure students' physical, social-emotional, developmental, and academic needs are being met.

---

2 Problem-solving conferences allow a student to collaborate with the teacher to come up with personalized solutions to problem behavior.

---

3 Class meetings bring the whole class together to brainstorm solutions to problems that affect the whole group.

---

4 Develop a positive relationship with parents early, and when you need to contact them about problem behavior, make it clear that you like and want to help their child, keep the conversation focused on the facts, and maintain a positive tone.

Managing the Effects of Toxic Stress

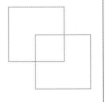

Managing the Effects of Toxic Stress

As discussed in Chapter 3, logical consequences can be a productive and effective way of dealing with many types of misbehavior. However, for some students experiencing a high degree of stress on an ongoing basis, the world doesn't always seem like a logical place. For example, in a home where physical abuse occurs, the abuser might lash out without warning or reason. Students who regularly experience intense stress may develop a type of severe stress response known as toxic stress. The physical and emotional changes associated with toxic stress can also make students behave in ways that may sometimes appear illogical. For instance, a gentle and well-intentioned bit of feedback on an assignment might be taken as an insult, and the student might get defiant or run off in self-defense.

This chapter will examine how toxic stress influences students' minds, bodies, and behavior in the classroom. Healthy and consistent relationships with supportive adults can be a stabilizing influence for students experiencing toxic stress, and this chapter offers strategies for forging those relationships and creating a safe, predictable learning community. In addition, you'll find information on addressing outbursts and other behavioral issues that may result from toxic stress.

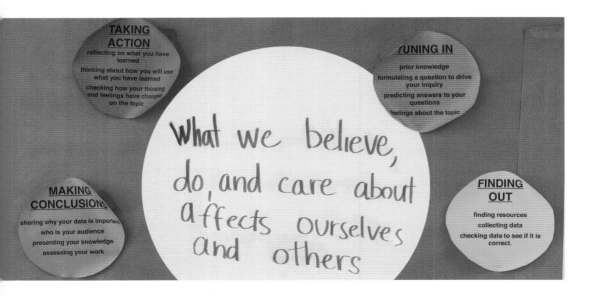

ealthy Stress vs. Toxic Stress

Researchers at Harvard's Center on the Developing Child (n.d.) outline three levels of stress responses that young people may experience. Minor to moderate stress affects all adolescents sometimes just like it affects all adults. A student may worry about a test they're about to take, feel anxious about starting school in a new town, or become startled at the sound of the fire alarm. These sorts of situations provoke a stress response that raise a student's stress hormone levels, blood pressure, and heart rate. These physical changes allow a person to go into "fight, flight, or freeze" mode to escape predators or other dangers—all part of a healthy stress response that has evolved in human beings to help us survive hazardous situations. Because situations like these are limited in scope, levels quickly return to baseline.

A second type of stress response, known as tolerable stress, occurs when the stressors are more extreme. These can include traumas like being affected by a natural disaster or losing a loved one. Events like these activate the body's physical and chemical stress responses to a higher degree and push the body beyond a healthy stress response. However, if the scope of the event is limited in time and adequate support from adults is available, a young adolescent can fully recover from this type of stress response (Changing Minds, n.d.-a).

But when a young person experiences stressful events on a regular or ongoing basis and does not have adequate support from the adults around them, they may experience a toxic stress response. This can happen to students from all backgrounds and may result from a wide variety of causes, some of which include abuse, neglect, repeated exposure to violence in the home or community, a parent's addiction or chronic illness, poverty, and systemic discrimination. Students living in these circumstances may remain on high alert, vigilant for warning signs that they need to protect themselves. Because of this, they may be more likely to go into fight, flight, or freeze mode even in areas of their life where their stressors are not present, such as school. For example, an acquaintance giving a friendly tap on the shoulder to get a student's attention might be misconstrued as that person trying to start a physical fight.

From the outside, these students may simply appear to be acting out. But on the inside, they are doing their best to survive, and they are doing so under the influence of stress hormones that make it challenging for them to control their behavior. These elevated stress hormone levels can, over time, damage students' brains and other organs, leading to higher risks of physical and mental illnesses such as heart disease, depression, and substance abuse. This flood of stress hormones can also negatively affect cognitive development, creating fewer neural connections to areas of the brain that control behavior regulation, and more connections to those areas associated with impulsiveness and anxiety.

Fortunately, we as teachers can have a positive impact on students who are experiencing toxic stress. Forming healthy, steady relationships with adults can reduce these risks and prevent or even reverse some damage caused by heightened stress levels. Once a positive and supportive relationship has been established, something as simple as a kind word or act from a trusted adult can release brain chemicals that promote bonding, empathy, and trust. This can have a significant impact on a student's ability to feel safe and supported. The strategies in this chapter offer numerous ways to build these relationships and support students experiencing toxic stress.

Fortunately, we as teachers can have a positive impact on students who are experiencing toxic stress.

Supporting Students Who Are Experiencing Toxic Stress

The *Responsive Classroom* approach to supporting students experiencing toxic stress is built on six "pillars":

- Provide an emotionally safe school and classroom

- Model respectfulness

- Explicitly teach social and emotional skills

- Incorporate playfulness into learning

- Communicate hope

- Foster your own self-care and build a supportive community

For each of these six pillars, you'll find tips and techniques to help you build a foundation of support for all students in the class, and particularly those experiencing toxic stress. Within this healthy learning environment, students are more likely to feel safe and find success as they build important social and emotional skills.

Provide an Emotionally Safe School and Classroom

Having strong connections with adults can help students feel a sense of safety and predictability within the school environment, helping to lessen the chances of students going into fight, flight, or freeze mode. It also creates an atmosphere where students feel valued and comfortable taking academic risks. These effects can increase students' academic engagement and bolster their mental and physical well-being.

The *Responsive Classroom* practices of Responsive Advisory Meeting and closing the day are both strong ways to build a safe and supportive classroom community. These predictable routines contribute to a sense of stability and allow students experiencing toxic stress regular opportunities to build connections with their peers and teachers and strengthen their sense of belonging. Welcoming students' self-expression through the components of Responsive Advisory Meeting and the brief discussions held while closing the day tells students that you care about what they have to say and builds the groundwork for students to put their trust in you. These regular routines support students as they transition into and out of the school day, and can also be used to discuss situations that may increase students' stress, such as upcoming testing or current events that are on their minds.

Brain breaks are another tool you can use to support students dealing with toxic stress. These quick, whole class activities are designed to refresh students' brains and bodies to help them feel focused and alert. They also offer safe and structured opportunities for connection and engagement as a group, and are fast and easy to work into the class period. Refocusing brain breaks can be especially useful, as they provide chances throughout the day to decrease stress—especially important for students experiencing toxic stress, but beneficial for all other students, as well.

One important way to create predictability in your classroom is by using Interactive Modeling (see pages 28–32) to teach students the various procedures they need to know how to do. By setting clear expectations that students can understand and follow, you help create a safe and orderly environment where everyone knows what to do and when and how to do it.

Along with the above strategies, here are some tips for creating a safe and predictable learning community where students feel comfortable creating strong connections with their peers and with you:

- **Be a good listener.** When having one-on-one conversations with a student who is experiencing toxic stress, find a private place where distractions are minimal. Let the student decide if and when they want to share their feelings with you. When a student is ready to talk, make sure to listen without interrupting. Also, be prepared to talk through difficult experiences more than once, since toxic stress is the result of challenges that students will need time and support to process. If they need additional support to make sense of what they've experienced, connect them with a school counselor or another professional who can help.

IN THE CLASSROOM

Mr. Abdus-Salaam

Students who are experiencing toxic stress need to know someone cares about them, which is one of the reasons Mr. Abdus-Salaam finds it so important to get to know students and build a strong rapport right from the beginning of the year. He does his best to open up a dialogue with students who are struggling, and he has found that students truly do want to be heard. For some students, he finds it helpful to have a "daily debrief" to chat for a few minutes about how things are going, both personally and academically. This reinforces the feeling he wants to create that the classroom is a community where everyone is heard and supported.

- **Ask open-ended questions to encourage students to express themselves.** Stay open to hearing students' thoughts, ideas, and concerns, which you can draw out through open-ended questions. Be curious and nonjudgmental while listening—for example, instead of asking, "Why did you talk back to me when I gave the class directions?" ask, "What were you feeling when I gave the class directions?" Paraphrase what they tell you to make sure you understand them correctly and to show them that you're listening.

- **Think about what your body language is communicating.** To show students you're actively listening, make friendly eye contact, maintain an open posture, and nod in acknowledgment at what they are saying.

- **Demonstrate your trustworthiness.** Build trust with students by upholding your word and following through on any promises you make, and by remaining calm and kind in the face of any outbursts.

- **Make the Space and Time areas comfortable.** Include a spot with comfortable seating and soothing decorations, and also give students the option to stand or stretch if they prefer. Also, provide tools such as stress balls or notepads they can use to help them calm down while they're there. Be sure to teach students through Interactive Modeling how to use Space and Time (see pages 71–75), and consistently frame this practice as one that benefits students by helping them learn self-control and feel relaxed and ready to learn.

To learn more about the practices mentioned in this section, see:

The Responsive Advisory Meeting Book: 150+ Purposeful Plans for Middle School (Center for Responsive Schools, 2018)

Refocus and Recharge! 50 Brain Breaks for Middle Schoolers (Center for Responsive Schools, 2016)

Building an Academic Community: The Middle School Teacher's Guide to the First Four Weeks of the School Year (Center for Responsive Schools, 2018)

Model Respectfulness

All students need to feel respected in the classroom to achieve their greatest potential and have a sense of well-being, but it's especially important for students experiencing toxic stress (Cohen, Cardillo, and Pickeral 2011). Such students may be more inclined than others to misinterpret innocent interactions as disrespectful, and may act out when they're feeling disrespected (Tough 2016). By displaying respect toward all students and encouraging respect among them, you can help students experiencing toxic stress feel calmer and safer, lowering the chances that their fight, flight, or freeze mode will kick in.

Respect means more than just acting courteously to one another. We must show students that we are listening to them and taking them seriously, and build a classroom environment in which all students do the same for their peers. Getting to know students as individuals, giving everyone a voice, and showing genuine curiosity for their thoughts and ideas are all important ways to cultivate a climate of respect. Giving students guided choices about what to learn, how to learn it, or both is another way to demonstrate respect toward our students. This practice gives students autonomy and signals that you respect them as independent learners and decision makers. When a student looks for help or feedback, showing empathy and patience toward them can indicate that you are invested in what they are trying to accomplish.

Teacher language also plays a critical role in modeling respectfulness. By letting students know what they are doing well, reinforcing language (see pages 23–24) strengthens your relationship with students and deepens their trust in you by showing that you respect their skills and effort. Reinforcing language can also build students' confidence in their own abilities, and subsequently, their sense of self-respect.

When students start to get off task, reminding language (see pages 24–25) gives you the opportunity to show that you believe in their ability to refocus and make good choices. In order for reminding language to convey respect, it's essential to be aware of tone, word choice, and body language. Especially when directing reminding language at students experiencing toxic stress, use reminders that are calm, direct, and focused on the behavior rather than the student's character. Also, before using reminding language, be sure that expectations are clear, having been explicitly taught and modeled in your classroom.

In addition to modeling respectfulness yourself, you can reinforce respectful behavior in your classroom by teaching and having students practice cooperation skills. Cooperation skills help students work productively with one another and manage conflicts respectfully. These skills are vital for students experiencing toxic stress, who may struggle to connect with others. Here are some tips for helping students develop these skills:

■ **Create opportunities for students to work with their peers toward a common goal.** A guiding principle of the *Responsive Classroom* approach is that great cognitive growth occurs through social interaction. Students who are experiencing toxic stress may need extra support in learning to work well with others, so having ample opportunities to practice these skills is vital.

■ **Teach and model how groups can work together** to solve problems by brainstorming possible solutions, sharing and assessing those ideas, and choosing one to try (for example, through class meetings; see pages 96–98).

■ **Help students control their emotions and work through obstacles.** Guide students as they build the skills they need to anticipate challenges, deal with them when they occur, seek help when stuck, share opinions respectfully, and manage feelings of frustration in healthy ways when they arise.

■ **Identify other sources of support.** Help students find adults in the school or wider community who can provide additional or specialized support and guidance, such as counselors or community advocates. Also help students locate other sources of help, if needed, such as local support groups.

Explicitly Teach Social and Emotional Skills

One of the main consequences of toxic stress is that it can cause students to easily lose control and instinctively go into fight, flight, or freeze mode. Thus, these students need support and time to practice controlling their impulses. Fortunately, classroom life is full of opportunities for practicing self-control and for learning to regulate one's thoughts, emotions, and behaviors.

Role-playing (see pages 33–34) can help students practice healthy behavior in challenging academic and social situations. This technique offers a safe and structured way to think about appropriate ways to act through the use of low-stakes, made-up scenarios. As you watch students practice social-emotional skills in these scenarios, think about which students may need individual support in further developing these skills. And as you see students try out these skills in actual classroom life, reinforce the progress they make to bolster their confidence and help them build on their growing abilities.

When students become stressed and you notice them showing signs that they are struggling with self-control, visual and verbal cues and teacher proximity (see pages 57–58) can help them get back on task. These techniques show that you're paying attention and believe in their ability to meet expectations. And because they minimize the amount of attention drawn to the student, they are respectful of young adolescents who can easily become uncomfortable when they feel put on the spot—particularly those who experience toxic stress and may lash out or withdraw when they feel self-conscious.

If a student is not able to regain self-control and their actions escalate to misbehavior, you might try using logical consequences (see pages 65–80). While they may not work in every situation, logical consequences can sometimes provide support for a student who has lost control and can show them what self-control would look like in this situation. Showing students how to calmly fix something they've broken, put aside a privilege they're not using responsibly, or take Space and Time to calm down can help them get back on task and see how they might be more successful next time. (If a student's actions have moved beyond ordinary misbehavior and have reached the level of a full-blown outburst, see pages 121–125 for strategies to try.)

◼ IN THE CLASSROOM

Mr. Moral

In addition to using Space and Time in his classroom, Mr. Moral uses a support he calls "take a walk." This is a specific practice that he teaches and models at the beginning of the year so that students know exactly what to do: leave the classroom quietly, walk to the water fountain at the end of the hallway, and then return within one minute. This practice provides a useful alternative when students become too self-conscious or are otherwise unable to get what they need from Space and Time. Taking a brief walk in a structured way lets students know they have an opportunity to calm down safely and privately.

As you think about ways to teach social-emotional skills to students experiencing toxic stress, here are some ideas to consider:

- **Help students talk about their feelings and translate their emotions into words.** If you notice from a student's body language or facial expression that they seem sad, frustrated, or angry, help them identify and name those emotions. Encourage them to talk about their feelings with you or another trusted adult.

- **Help students express their emotions** in safe and creative ways, such as through writing, music, or art. Take their feelings seriously even if their concerns seem minor to you.

- **Work with students to anticipate challenges they may face.** As you consider upcoming projects and assignments, talk with students about obstacles that may arise and brainstorm possible solutions together. Role-playing (see pages 33–34) may be adapted for one-on-one use to test these solutions out if the student is comfortable using the technique that way. They might also freewrite about possible obstacles and outcomes, or they could try storyboarding or drawing comics to help them see, step by step, how a situation may unfold.

- **Teach students problem-solving skills for a variety of situations.** Students need the skills to respond to all sorts of situations, from coming to a consensus within a group to solving a difficult math problem on their own. Guide them through this work and support their efforts, but let them find the answer themselves. Give them credit for working to solve a problem even if they are not completely successful in doing so.

- **When students are calm, teach them skills** they can use when stress levels begin to rise. Meditation or deep-breathing techniques, stretches, and tactile grounding techniques like standing with their back pressed against a wall are all useful skills that can be taught through Interactive Modeling. Students can employ these techniques on their own in a range of situations, such as while in Space and Time, while sitting at their desk, or when at home. Help students learn to recognize their own signals that their stress levels are rising so that they can quickly take steps to maintain self-control.

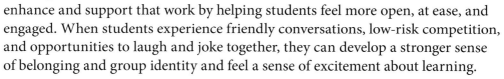

Incorporate Playfulness Into Learning

A sense of playfulness in the classroom can help students feel more comfortable and creative in their learning. Not only can playfulness coexist with the serious and important work of school but it can enhance and support that work by helping students feel more open, at ease, and engaged. When students experience friendly conversations, low-risk competition, and opportunities to laugh and joke together, they can develop a stronger sense of belonging and group identity and feel a sense of excitement about learning.

In addition to supporting a friendly and engaging classroom community, play serves an important role in students' emotional development. It can help reduce stress in the moment and improve students' ability to cope with stress in the long term. Playfulness is a mood, not a fixed personality characteristic, which means that with our help, students experiencing toxic stress can develop and grow their playfulness over time. By incorporating play throughout the school day, we can help these students feel more connected to school and their community of peers, and more comfortable participating in academics.

Brain breaks are an excellent way to bring playfulness into the classroom. In addition to supporting all students' physical and social needs and helping their brains prepare for learning, brain breaks help all students feel a sense of joy and connection. As you try out different brain breaks with a class, notice which ones they seem to enjoy the most. Finding and repeating class favorites is a great way to build community and a sense of shared identity. Also keep an eye out for how students experiencing toxic stress are responding to a particular activity. If a student is too self-conscious or is otherwise hesitant to participate, find lower-risk ways to involve them at first, such as by having them observe and make notes on what they saw. Later, they can participate more fully as they grow to feel comfortable doing so.

Playfulness can be incorporated into lessons and transition periods throughout the school day. Here are some ideas for boosting fun and engagement for all students, including those experiencing toxic stress:

- **Maintain a sense of humor.** Look for and share the humor in challenging moments when appropriate, and show students you can laugh at your own mistakes. You can also bring out the lighter side of your academic content by having students write riddles or jokes that incorporate vocabulary words or figures of speech, historical figures and facts, scientific terms, or other academic information.

- **Encourage creative play.** Give students opportunities to produce skits, songs, drawings, board games, or comic strips about what they're learning—whatever gets them excited to engage with academic content.

- **Play on students' natural inquisitiveness.** Give students the chance to follow their own curiosity as they engage with and explore new content. Choosing their own research topics or reading materials, going on field trips, and doing science experiments all offer opportunities for students to formulate their own questions and find their own answers.

 To learn more about brain breaks, see *Refocus and Recharge! 50 Brain Breaks for Middle Schoolers* (Center for Responsive Schools, 2016).

Communicate Hope

Hope means more than simply being optimistic. It's a cognitive process that, like all social and emotional skills, can be learned and practiced. C. R. Snyder's (1994) theory of hope tells us that this process revolves around an individual having goals, pursuing those goals, and believing that they are capable of achieving them. This can be challenging for students experiencing toxic stress, who may struggle to envision a positive future for themselves. You can help these students build their sense of hope for the future by recognizing and nurturing their unique talents and showing them that you believe in their potential.

Envisioning language (see page 22) is one of the most influential tools we have to help students develop their sense of hope. Naming positive identities and outcomes for students helps them picture their future successes, which supports them in aiming high, meeting their goals, and building their confidence. These outcomes may be as small and immediate as successfully completing an assignment due the next day, or as large and far-off as a career goal. In either case, envisioning language aims to help students see what they are capable of achieving.

Giving students choices about what and how they learn can also help students develop a sense of hope. Providing guided options supports students as it empowers them to build their own vision of their academic future. This practice also invites them to become more engaged in figuring out what their ideal learning process looks like.

Here are some additional tips to help you build a stronger sense of hope in the students you teach:

- **Help students set short- and long-term goals.** Whether they're setting goals to work toward over the next week or over the entire year, help students break those goals down into achievable steps. Work with students to develop the skills they need to achieve their goals, including ways to handle obstacles or seek help when they get stuck. Along the way, reinforce their efforts and help them brainstorm solutions to any problems that stand in their way.

- **Promote positive risk-taking.** Offer opportunities to take academic and social risks in a safe environment, such as leading a group activity or initiating a conversation with someone they don't know well. When students make mistakes in their academic work or social interactions, frame those mistakes as a normal part of the learning process. Guide students in reflecting on their errors as a way of helping them figure out what to do differently next time.

- **Nurture students' creativity and curiosity.** Give students opportunities to express their creativity through the arts, try out activities that interest them, and explore topics that intrigue them academically. Help them connect their interests to afterschool programs or other activities in the community when possible, and discuss ways in which their developing interests could lead to various career paths.

- **Use fiction or stories about real people as a springboard** to discuss how people have worked hard and faced many different types of obstacles on the road to success. These people might be fictional characters, or they might be community leaders or famous scientists, writers, musicians, or athletes. Talk to students about who their role models are and why they admire them, and help them see what those role models may have had to overcome to get where they are today.

- **Help students see themselves as valuable members of your academic community.** Give students the chance to take on leadership roles in the classroom, such as by helping you label and organize supplies, or in the wider school community, such as by being a guide to show new students around the school.

- **Talk about the qualities of a good friend.** Help students understand what it means to be a good friend to others, and discuss ways to find peers who will be good friends to them. Emphasize the importance of making authentic connections with others and making friends with people who believe in them.

- **Recognize the challenges in students' lives.** Help students experiencing toxic stress envision healthy and productive ways to manage the challenges they face, and reinforce their efforts in adapting and surviving.

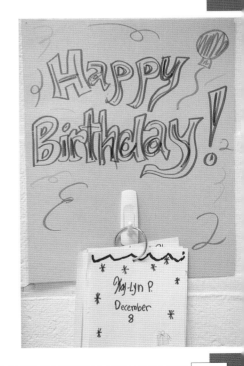

- **Help all students celebrate their accomplishments and unique abilities.** When a student has a success, even a small one, give them genuine reinforcing feedback. For students experiencing toxic stress, take extra care to reinforce successes in the areas of connecting with others, taking healthy risks, and showing perseverance in challenging situations.

- **Remember and recognize special occasions,** such as students' birthdays or any events they've been looking forward to, such as a big sports game or a school exhibition of student artwork.

Foster Your Own Self-Care
and Build a Supportive Community

As teachers, we give a great deal of ourselves to students, and self-care can sometimes get lost in the shuffle. We may not even realize just how much time and energy we've spent on others until we find that we're exhausted and stressed out. It's essential to take time for self-care, most importantly in order to remain physically, mentally, and emotionally healthy and well-balanced, but also to be able to continue giving to the students we teach. Students experiencing toxic stress may need higher amounts of support and attention, and our empathy for these students may mean that we share in their emotional burden. It's critical to take care of ourselves and find the support we need, particularly if many of the students we teach are affected by toxic stress or are especially prone to outbursts.

If you are part of a teaching team, work together to strategize how to help any students on the team who experience toxic stress. What warning signs have you noticed when a student is about to lose self-control? What methods have worked so far in helping a particular student who is having an outburst or withdrawing emotionally or physically during class? These discussions can not only help you brainstorm effective ways to help students and share your knowledge but can also help ensure a consistent and compassionate response to a student from all members of the teaching team. If you are not part of an established team, consider forming your own team with other teachers (such as a group of elective teachers coming together for regular meetings). Other professionals in the school, such as principals, guidance counselors, or paraprofessionals, may also be useful sources of support. Stay in touch with them throughout the year about the students in your class so that they will be ready to assist in the moment of an outburst and to debrief with you afterward.

Spending time and energy on your own growth and well-being is just as important as spending time and energy helping students grow. This is especially true if you have experienced trauma yourself, in which case seeing what students are going through might trigger your own difficult memories or emotions. Just like the students you teach, you need to give yourself time, space, and empathy to heal. Even if you haven't personally experienced significant trauma, helping students who are experiencing the ongoing effects of toxic stress can take its toll. This effect, known as secondary traumatic stress, compassion fatigue, or empathic distress, can induce feelings of anger, guilt, and hopelessness, and may lead to social withdrawal, trouble sleeping, increased susceptibility to poor health, and feelings of isolation (National Child Traumatic Stress Network, n.d.). These symptoms should be taken seriously, and we must remember that seeking help is a sign of strength, not weakness. Finding ways to manage your stress can help you avoid burnout, remain healthy, and maintain a positive attitude about teaching (Changing Minds, n.d.-b).

These ideas can help you take care of yourself and be proactive about self-care:

- **Pay attention to your emotional health.** Make an effort to notice how your body feels when you're under stress so that you can identify your own signals that you need to calm down. Meditation, deep breathing, and other relaxation techniques can be useful both in a stressful moment and as a regular practice to help you stay balanced. You may also find it useful to speak to a therapist or other mental health professional, especially if you're struggling to help students experiencing toxic stress or if their challenges are bringing up your own difficult feelings.

- **Maintain good habits for your physical health.** When life gets hectic or stressful, the first things we often neglect are exercise, sleep, and a balanced diet. However, maintaining good habits for our health allows us to feel better not only physically but emotionally, and helps us focus and keep our composure in the face of stressful situations.

- **Celebrate your successes, no matter how small.** Keep a running list of moments you're proud of as a teacher. These can be anything from organizing a major school event to the look on a student's face when something you've taught them finally clicks in their mind. Turn to this list on challenging days when you need a morale boost. Also, compliment your colleagues on what you see them doing well. Doing so can help you stay positive and can also help create community among educators. Lean on them when you need someone to work through a challenge with, or if you simply need a chance to chat and relax.

- **Think about ways to make your classroom space feel welcoming.** Not only should your classroom feel comfortable and inviting to students but it should feel that way to you as well. Is the room decorated in a way that suits your personality? Do you have a comfortable chair to sit in? What personal touches can you add that will make your day brighter? Look for ways to stay connected to the things that matter most to you, such as by decorating your desk with photographs of people and places you love, items you or the people you care about have made, or framed notes from former students.

- **Keep a positive outlook.** Think about why you first decided to become a teacher. Consider incorporating this inspiration into a poem or a piece of art to hang in your classroom to keep yourself motivated. Find time to spend with people who make you feel happy and energized.

- **Think about your work-life balance.** Make time for your interests and hobbies, including new ones that you've always wanted to try. Volunteering for a beloved cause, joining an athletic team or taking a fun exercise class, and pursuing your creative interests are all good ways to stay in a joyful and balanced state of mind.

By making an effort to practice good self-care, you are first and foremost taking care of yourself, which you need and deserve. In addition, you are showing the students you teach what it looks like to prioritize one's own well-being. For students experiencing toxic stress who may not have much experience seeing healthy coping mechanisms in action, you are providing an invaluable example and helping them to envision a healthier future for themselves.

Responding to Outbursts and Withdrawal

Students experiencing toxic stress may constantly be on the lookout for subtle signs of danger—for example, listening for changes in a parent's voice that indicate they're getting angry or are under the influence of drugs. This hypervigilance is a natural adaptation to ongoing stressful circumstances. Because of this adaptation, students experiencing toxic stress may have a heightened fight, flight, or freeze mode impulse, which can be triggered during school for reasons that may not be immediately obvious to us. This may look like:

- **Fight**—a student having a verbal outburst, becoming defiant, or physically lashing out against a teacher or another student

- **Flight**—a student running out of the classroom or walking away from a learning activity to a different part of the room

- **Freeze**—a student becoming overwhelmed by sensory information when under stress and disengaging from learning in the classroom

No matter which of these scenarios unfolds, the student's need is the same: for a trusted adult to help them calm down and regain self-control. In order to do this, we must maintain empathy and compassion. Handling outbursts and withdrawal in a sensitive and caring way gives these students what they need and contributes to an environment where everyone feels safe. It also avoids the risks of using harsher, more punitive approaches, such as yelling at the student or suspending them, which can exacerbate the situation and make all students feel unsafe. Such harsh approaches can also lead to a negative cycle in which a student has an outburst, is removed from the classroom, and falls behind in their academic work, causing the student to become even more frustrated and disconnected from the class and leading to the potential for more outbursts. By handling outbursts and withdrawal in a more positive way, you can help all students stay on track and feel safe in your classroom.

Before an Outburst or Other Incident

Knowing students and their needs is always important, and especially so with students experiencing toxic stress. Paying attention and learning what factors may lead to an outburst or withdrawal can help you avoid or minimize such situations. Similarly, discovering an individual student's warning signs that they're about to lose self-control can help you guide them and get them what they need to calm down before the situation escalates.

You can build this knowledge through observation of and conversations with your students. If an outburst or withdrawal does occur, take time later to reflect on how the student was behaving immediately before the incident so that you will be better able to recognize their signals next time. Also think about what was or wasn't effective in helping them get back in control, and which of the student's peers are more likely to calm them or to set them off.

You may find useful strategies for stopping a potential outburst in the six pillars discussed in this chapter. You might also try visual and verbal cues and teacher proximity (see pages 57–58) to help a student maintain self-control when you see their warning signs appear. Establishing an individual signal in advance with that student can also be a good way of showing that you're paying attention, helping them recognize their own warning signs, and letting them know you're there to help them if they need it.

In some cases, leaving the situation is an important way to help a student avoid becoming overly stressed and going into fight, flight, or freeze mode. Space and Time (see pages 71–75) can be helpful, but it's important to first establish it as a nonpunitive resource that everyone uses. As you continue working with students experiencing toxic stress, encourage them to take Space and Time when they feel they need it. Doing so shows your trust in them and helps them build self-confidence as well as supporting them in learning their own signals and controlling their own feelings. Sometimes, it may be appropriate to allow a student to leave the room for a few minutes. Sending them to get a drink of water from the fountain or run an errand for you gives them a structured way to take a moment away from the class to collect themselves.

Responding to Outbursts in the Moment

When an outburst does occur, your primary responsibility is to regain control of the situation to ensure that everyone in the classroom, including the student having the outburst, is safe. The best way to go about this will depend on the student and their needs. You may need to move the student to a different part of the room, bring them into the hall and do a deep breathing exercise together, or distract them from the situation. As you get to know the students you teach, you will develop a better sense of what a particular student might need.

It isn't appropriate to try and discuss the student's behavior in the moment of the outburst. Research shows that the part of the brain focused on survival instincts and emotional memory, the amygdala, can overtake the "thinking" mind, the prefrontal cortex, during times of stress (Goleman 1995). Because of this takeover, sometimes known as "amygdala hijack," the student won't be able to think rationally while in fight, flight, or freeze mode. As a result, any conversations about the student's behavior should wait until they've regained self-control and their stress level has receded.

If you haven't already done so, sending the student to Space and Time may help them calm down during an outburst. However, take particular care to send them in a discreet way, as making them feel self-conscious may escalate defiance. Now might also be a good time to call on a counselor or other professional in the school who can work with the student and help them calm down, perhaps by going with them on a walk around the building or to an area where they can take a moment to refocus. A counselor's office, designated cool-down room, or a quiet corner in the building may provide the reprieve from stressful sensory information that the student needs. Stay in touch with these colleagues throughout the school year so that they will be up-to-date on the student's needs and challenges and will understand their role should you need their assistance.

When dealing with an outburst, it's especially important to keep your tone of voice calm. A composed, sincere demeanor shows everyone in the classroom that you are maintaining control of the situation, which will help all students feel safe. It also signals to the student having the outburst that you are genuinely interested in helping them, whereas a flustered or angry tone might come across as threatening, which can escalate the situation further. Minimizing the number of words you use during an outburst will help the student, whose cognitive thinking skills have been overwhelmed by stress hormones, to understand your directions. Saying less also allows you to focus on listening rather than talking so that you can gather information on how best to assist the student.

One of the most challenging, but most essential, things you can do for a student who is having an outburst is to maintain empathy for them. While the anger or insults that can happen during an outburst may feel personal, strive to remember that the student's behavior is a defensive mechanism as their brain and body go into survival mode.

> One of the most challenging, but most essential, things you can do for a student who is having an outburst is to maintain empathy for them.

Responding in a kind and discreet way minimizes the attention drawn to the behavior and tells the student that you respect their privacy. Framing your language to be curious rather than accusatory—"What's happening?" rather than "What's wrong with you?"—lets the student know you are on their side and want to help.

IN THE CLASSROOM

Mr. Moral

When a student is struggling due to toxic stress, Mr. Moral tries to find out as much as he can about them. He seeks this information from a variety of sources: the student's family, social workers or counselors who have worked with them, previous teachers, and the student themselves. Doing so helps him understand any additional considerations that will help him support the student.

In some cases, Mr. Moral seeks outside help in supporting a student, such as through a social worker, a guidance counselor, or the principal. If such a referral is necessary, he talks to the student about it to let them know what's happening. He frames these referrals in a way that focuses on his abilities to get the student what they need to help them regain self-control, not on any weakness on the student's part.

If, during an outburst, you find that you are unable to respond calmly and empathetically, have a member of your teaching team, guidance counselor, or other colleague take over until you have regained your composure. Remember, just like students, we also sometimes need a moment to cool off and regain self-control.

After the Student Has Cooled Down

Once an outburst has passed and the student has calmed down and regained self-control, have a private, nonjudgmental conversation about what happened. Ask for their input about what may have caused them to feel threatened, what emotions they may have been experiencing, and what might help them calm down next time. The student's responses can help you better understand their behavior, needs, and warning signs, and can also help the student put their feelings into words—an important skill that many students experiencing toxic stress need support in building. This conversation can also be a chance for you to teach the student other skills for calming down when they notice their stress levels rising, such as meditation, deep breathing, or focusing on physical sensations as a way to feel grounded.

You can also ask what support the student would like from you in helping them avoid outbursts or shutting down, or in helping them regain control. Listen seriously to any ideas the student offers about the kind of support they need, and if they aren't sure, offer some suggestions and see what they respond to. In addition, turn to behavior specialists, social workers, or other experts at your school, along with other teachers who have worked with the student, for advice on how to best support the student going forward.

Managing the Effects of Toxic Stress

1 When students experience extreme and prolonged trauma, they may develop a toxic stress response, which can have negative effects on their health, relationships, and behavior in school.

2 A six-pillar approach can help teachers support students experiencing toxic stress: provide an emotionally safe school and classroom, model respectfulness, explicitly teach social and emotional skills, incorporate playfulness into learning, communicate hope, and foster your own self-care and build a supportive community.

3 Toxic stress can make students more likely to have outbursts or to withdraw, but teachers can support students by identifying and avoiding triggers; staying calm during incidents; and helping students learn skills to express emotions, work with others, and calm themselves down when they start to feel out of control.

References

Center on the Developing Child of Harvard University. n.d. "Toxic Stress." Accessed June 13, 2018. https://developingchild.harvard.edu/science/key-concepts/toxic-stress/.

Centers for Disease Control and Prevention. n.d. "Adverse Childhood Experiences." Accessed June 13, 2018. https://www.cdc.gov/violenceprevention/acestudy.

Changing Minds. n.d.-a. "Gestures That Can Heal." Accessed June 13, 2018. https://changingmindsnow.org/healing.

Changing Minds. n.d.-b. "Taking Care of Yourself Helps You Take Care of Children." Accessed June 13, 2018. https://changingmindsnow.org/docs/Taking_Care_of_Yourself.pdf.

Cohen, Jonathan, Richard Cardillo, and Terry Pickeral. 2011. "Creating a Climate of Respect." *Educational Leadership* 69, no. 1 (September). http://www.ascd.org/publications/educational-leadership/sept11/vol69/num01/Creating-a-Climate-of-Respect.aspx.

Goleman, Daniel. 1995. *Emotional Intelligence: Why It Can Matter More Than IQ.* New York: Bantam Books.

National Child Traumatic Stress Network. n.d. "Secondary Traumatic Stress." Accessed June 13, 2018. http://www.nctsn.org/resources/topics/secondary-traumatic-stress.

Snyder, C. R. 1994. *The Psychology of Hope: You Can Get There From Here.* New York: Free Press.

Tough, Paul. 2016. *Helping Children Succeed: What Works and Why.* New York: Houghton Mifflin Harcourt.

Further
Resources

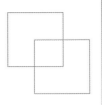

All the practices recommended in this book come from or are consistent with the *Responsive Classroom* approach to teaching—an evidence-based education approach associated with greater teacher effectiveness, higher student achievement, and improved school climate. *Responsive Classroom* practices help educators build competencies in four interrelated domains: engaging academics, positive community, effective management, and developmentally responsive teaching.

To learn more, see the following resources published by Center for Responsive Schools and available at www.responsiveclassroom.org.

Building an Academic Community: The Middle School Teacher's Guide to the First Four Weeks of the School Year (from *Responsive Classroom*, 2018). This book helps you use the energy of the first month of school to create a solid foundation for the entire year. Features practical information on managing the classroom, investing students in the rules, making the most of Advisory time, responding to misbehavior in productive ways, and more.

Middle School Motivators: 22 Interactive Learning Structures (from *Responsive Classroom*, 2016). These easy-to-use structures encourage all students to give their best effort, focus on learning goals, and collaborate effectively with one another in dynamic, purposeful, and respectful ways.

The Power of Our Words for Middle School: Teacher Language That Helps Students Learn (from *Responsive Classroom*, 2016). Practical information, tips, and examples for improving the professional language you use with students. Through your use of words and tone, you can more fully engage students in their learning and support positive development in all areas of their lives.

Refocus and Recharge: 50 Brain Breaks for Middle Schoolers (from *Responsive Classroom*, 2016). Quick, easy-to-learn activities that give students much-needed mental and physical breaks from rigorous learning, and increase their ability to stay on task and focus on the content you teach.

The Responsive Advisory Meeting Book: 150+ Purposeful Plans for Middle School (from *Responsive Classroom*, 2018). Use the combination of structure, purpose, and planning in this book to strengthen and enrich your Advisory meetings, providing students with a safe place to build respectful, trusting relationships with peers and adults, explore their interests, and develop new skills.

Yardsticks: Child and Adolescent Development Ages 4–14, 4th edition (by Chip Wood, 2017). This accessible reference concisely charts children's development, shows what behavior you can expect to see in the classroom (and at home) at different ages, and outlines ways you can support students' social-emotional and academic learning and growth.

Yardsticks Guide Series: Common Developmental Characteristics in the Classroom and at Home, Grades K–8 (from *Responsive Classroom*, 2018; based on *Yardsticks* by Chip Wood). Common characteristics of children's development are summarized in easy-to-scan, grade specific guides for educators and parents.

Publisher's Acknowledgments

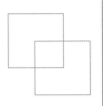

Center for Responsive Schools wishes to thank Rashid Abdus-Salaam, Andy Moral, and Kathleen Wylie for enriching this book by sharing their stories and their expertise. Thanks also to Joe Tilley, Amber Searles, Sarah Fillion, and Karen Poplawski for adding their thoughts and ideas to the conversation.

More than thirty years in the making, the *Responsive Classroom* approach to teaching continues to evolve thanks to the thousands of educators whose hard work and dedication improves students' lives all around the world. Our gratitude goes out to everyone who undertakes this essential work.

Index

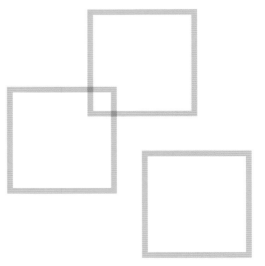

About the Publisher

Center for Responsive Schools, Inc., a not-for-profit educational organization, is the developer of *Responsive Classroom*®, an evidence-based education approach associated with greater teacher effectiveness, higher student achievement, and improved school climate. *Responsive Classroom* practices help educators build competencies in four interrelated domains: engaging academics, positive community, effective management, and developmentally responsive teaching. We offer the following resources for educators:

Professional Development Services

- Workshops for K–8 educators (locations around the country and internationally)

- On-site consulting services to support implementation

- Resources for site-based study

- Annual conferences for K–8 educators

Publications and Resources

- Books on a wide variety of *Responsive Classroom* topics

- Free monthly newsletter

- Extensive library of free articles on our website

For details, contact:

Center for Responsive Schools, Inc.
85 Avenue A, P.O. Box 718
Turners Falls, Massachusetts 01376-0718

800-360-6332   www.responsiveclassroom.org
info@responsiveclassroom.org

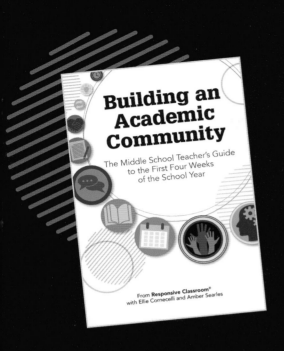

Specifications:

144 pages
7" x 10"
Paperback
Color

Each week, you'll find the building blocks to help you foster students' academic and social-emotional skills and develop a strong school community in which everyone can achieve their full potential!

Building an Academic Community

The Middle School Teacher's Guide to the First Four Weeks of the School Year

From *Responsive Classroom* with Ellie Cornecelli and Amber Searles

The first days of school are buzzing with excitement and questions as students meet new peers, start new routines, and look ahead to a year's worth of learning. This book shows you how to bring order and organization to the first month of school while maintaining the enthusiasm and curiosity students bring with them as they come back from summer vacation.

With individual chapters that address the first day and each of the first four weeks of the school year, this book offers practical information on:

→ Teaching the procedures and routines students need to be successful

→ Nurturing a healthy and productive learning community

→ Making the most of Advisory time

→ Introducing academic material and making lessons engaging

→ Helping students set goals and follow the rules in order to meet those goals

→ Effectively managing the classroom and other school spaces

→ Responding to misbehavior in constructive ways

To order or for more information, visit
www.responsiveclassroom.org

Responsive Classroom®

Find even more resources for middle school educators

Round out your library with these practical *Responsive Classroom* titles!

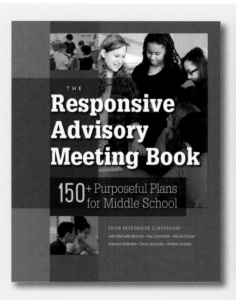

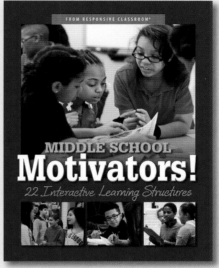

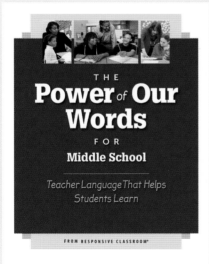

Responsive Classroom®

Introducing
Avenue A Books!

New from Center for Responsive Schools!

Avenue A Books offers a line of graphic novels that are specifically designed to help kids engage with the principles and competencies of social and emotional learning. This collection of engaging, colorful, and relevant books highlights real-world challenges that kids face at school and at home, helping them gain a deeper understanding of the situations they experience every day. The graphic novel format is perfect for both avid and reluctant readers—the use of images along with words provides an entertaining and dynamic reading experience, and can be an extremely effective way of communicating complex ideas and situations. These books offer subtle examples of how to handle tricky situations with empathy and self-control, and their compelling stories and attractive illustrations make them fun to read.

Learn more and sign up for new product updates at
www.avenueabooks.org